Caulerpa Conquest

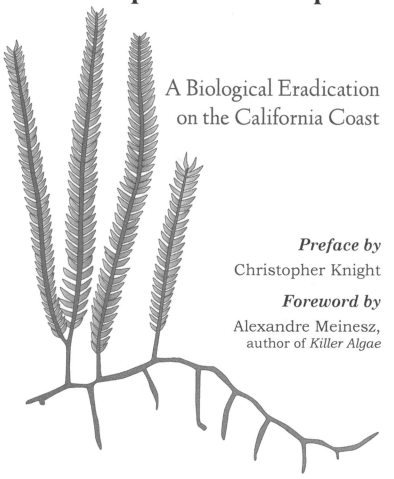

A Biological Eradication
on the California Coast

Preface by
Christopher Knight

Foreword by
Alexandre Meinesz,
author of *Killer Algae*

Eric Noel Muñoz

Open Books Press
Bloomington, Indiana

Published by Open Books Press, USA

www.OpenBooksPress.com
info@OpenBooksPress.com

An imprint of Pen & Publish, Inc.
www.PenandPublish.com
Bloomington, Indiana
(314) 827-6567

Print ISBN: 978-1-941799-42-0
eBook ISBN: 978-1-941799-43-7

Library of Congress Control Number: 2016946042

Caulerpa taxifolia chapter header image by Tracey Saxby,
IAN Image Library (ian.umces.edu/imagelibrary/)

Front cover photos by Eric Noel Muñoz:
Monaco Oceanographic Museum, 2015
Caulerpa taxifolia in water, Cap Ferrat, France, 2015
Carlsbad's Agua Hedionda Lagoon, 2013

Back cover photos:
Eric Muñoz with *Caulerpa taxifolia*, France, 2015 by Lizzie Muñoz
Agua Hedionda Lagoon Aerial by Google Earth
Caulerpa taxifolia Watchcard by sccat.net

Acknowledgments

For inspiring me to write this book I have to start by thanking the geography program at San Diego State University many years ago for adding a technical and educated component to my passion for caring about the coast and our oceans; to the members of the Southern California *Caulerpa* Action Team (SCCAT) including Lars Anderson, Bill Paznokas, Bob Hoffman, Bruce Posthumous, and his heroic predecessor Greig Peters; the Merkel team including Keith Merkel, the "queen of the lagoon" Rachel Woodfield, and Robert Mooney who provided huge value to my draft manuscript; David Lloyd of the power plant; members, staff, and fellow board directors of the Agua Hedionda Lagoon Foundation including Ken Alfrey, Steve LePage, and Al Cerda who served as vice presidents during my time as foundation president; scientists, media reporters, conference attendees, environmental coalitions; Croatian dive shop staff, Italian and Australian fishermen, Gold Coast city councillors, New Zealand city planners, and even Monaco Aquarium staff; the general public, and the countless local school children who were determined to solve environmental problems during the course of my presentations to them.

For converting my vision into a book and promoting the message of our *Caulerpa* Conquest, I thank Eli Enigenburg for our collaboration on the TED animated video; the concerned Carlsbad citizens who over time proved in many, unexpected ways their unwavering love for the health of Agua Hedionda Lagoon; the local surfers, paddlers, boaters, fishermen, and ocean lovers who always supported the eradication and outreach efforts; past and present city council members in Carlsbad and especially the late, great Mayor Claude "Bud" Lewis, and former city colleagues Ray Patchett, Ron Ball, Michael Holzmiller, and Don Rideout; to both my Hollywood and celebrity connection of David Mirisch and concerned Earth citizen Christopher Knight: our friendship is priceless. My hometown mates for their endless love and support: Roger

Donner, Marty Vlaco, John Saroyan, and of course, Rat and Twain. I also appreciate the support of Wendy Hinman of Carlsbad Magazine; Jim Kempton, President of the California Surf Museum; Jennifer Geist of Open Books Press; special gratitude to Daniel Simberloff of the University of Tennessee for carefully translating the foreword by Alexandre Meinesz from French into English; and for providing me excellent guidance and support: my editor, agent, and new friend Bob Yehling.

And a special note of appreciation to all the scientists, researchers, agency staff, and governmental officials from around the world, along the California coast, and specifically the incredible Mediterranean Sea. Thierry Thibaut of the Mediterranean Institute of Oceanography in Marseille, France, showed me an incredible amount of hospitality and time to educate and entertain me, along with his colleague Marc Verlaque. And finally, I have no way to extend a proper level of appreciation to Alexandre Meinesz. He unknowingly put my work into motion through his own experience of writing *Killer Algae*. This story of our *Caulerpa* Conquest is a tribute to the alarm he tried to raise in Mediterranean waters to which we somehow responded with a victorious outcome. His intelligence and raw love of the ocean is, for me, on a pedestal of unmatchable quality and integrity.

Eric Noel Muñoz • Carlsbad, California
July 2016

"We've all seen the movies where a monster created by scientists in a laboratory escapes to wreak havoc on the outside world. But what if the monster was not some giant rampaging beast destroying a city, but just a tiny amount of seaweed with the potential to disrupt entire coastal ecosystems. This is the story of *Caulerpa taxifolia* . . ."

—Opening excerpt from "Attack of the Killer Algae" by Eric Noel Muñoz,
TED-Ed video, June 24, 2014
ed.ted.com/lessons/attack-of-the-killer-algae-eric-noel-Muñoz

Lagoon and Ocean Community

To all the longtime Agua Hedionda Lagoon lovers and especially newer ones that may not realize how close our lagoon came to getting shut down; and also to ocean, wetland, and saltwater people around the world: treasure, protect, and enjoy what you have

Carlsbad Community

To all the local, underground, and pro surfers with a special mention to Scott Chandler, Carlsbad surf legend and community inspiration

Family

To my mom for being my life source and supporting my ocean relationship from early on; to my dad for challenging me to live with compassion, intelligence, and adventure; to my brothers Arturo and Jon and sister Laura for their love and for showing me different versions of how to live life; to my cousins Carlos, John, and Tom for showing me the signpost of a surfing life; and to my wife Isabelle (Lizzie) for everything

Contents

Foreword
Christopher Knight

Eric Muñoz's story of the eradication of "Killer Algae" from the Agua Hedionda Lagoon is a tribute to the vision and power of "individuals." It took many, many decisive people working together to win out over the silent green invasion of *Caulerpa taxifolia*. It was, after all, not just an enormous community effort, but a coordinated national, state, and local governmental, inter-agency endeavor with interest and support from the international scientific community. Yet, as it seems is always the case in stories with happy endings, the community needed an early champion and stalwart guardian. Somebody with the insight to understand the threat, the temperance and skill to communicate it, the humanity to inspire a call to action, and the wisdom to stay vigilant.

The entire community was brought together and rallied by an unlikely local hero whose love of the ocean, devotion to the environment, and passion for people caused him to be at the center of this success story. Eric Muñoz is the hero.

I entered the killer algae story at the culmination of the *Caulerpa taxifolia* plague. In May of 2008, I was invited down to Agua Hedionda with a group of celebrities to help memorialize the declaration that the lagoon's killer algae had been eradicated.

I live 90 miles north of the lagoon in Los Angeles, but was familiar with the three lagoons in North San Diego County from years of visiting the area. Having an interest in the environment and having grown up in LA since the late 1950s, I've become sensitive to how little natural habitat remains undeveloped. In my lifetime, nearly the entire Southern California region, save for mountainous areas, has been paved over. Yet, in all my years growing up and driving past the lagoons of San Diego County, they have remained uniquely natural. Even as millions of people have moved in and around them, they remain beautiful and environmentally productive.

Coastal wetlands in Southern California are rare. Most have been paved over or exploited for use as harbors and marinas. The remaining wetlands have remained undeveloped because we, the educated masses, began to understand their environmental importance and fragility. Wetlands are precious everywhere. As measured by their scarcity, they are seemingly more valuable here, in arid Southern California, than they are in any other place in the country. I've always been heartened to see that Carlsbad and the communities of North San Diego County saw fit to leave the lagoons alone.

Thus, I was an eager participant when asked to join with some celebrity friends in the Agua Hedionda Lagoon Foundation's first-ever fishing contest in celebration of the two-year anniversary of the *Caulerpa taxifolia* eradication. In all my years, I'd never actually been in or on the lagoon, though I had witnessed from the car window many people enjoying water sports whenever I'd be driving past on Interstate 5 toward San Diego.

It was then that I met Eric Muñoz and learned of the attack of the killer algae. I hadn't been aware of the lagoon's plight. It had been a long six-year battle, but outside of environmental circles and the local community, I'm not certain how many people actually knew that the lagoon had almost died as a functioning tidal estuary because of the invasive aquarium algae. However, I was aware by virtue of a television program I remembered watching on the Discovery Channel of the growing algae issue in the Mediterranean. Eric helped me connect the dots. He was my killer algae guide, and soon I was seeing what Eric and the Carlsbad community had accomplished and the stewardship they had provided.

All of us living in California, whose coastal waters could have been forever altered if the *Caulerpa* found its way out to the open coastal zone, owe them a giant debt of gratitude. This was a massive win. It was a giant man-made and ongoing disaster avoided, yet few outside of the local area, academia, and governmental agencies knew anything about it.

It was then that I began to understand Eric's concern. Getting people aligned when facing an impending disaster is far easier than trying to get them to align in advance to prevent it. It is only natural to think of a threat that has been overcome as passed. But as long as *Caulerpa taxifolia* is available for purchase for aquariums anywhere, there remains a chance it could be reintroduced into the local environment and repopulate all over again. Without outreach, without annual memorial celebrations, without noise reminding the community of the disaster that could have been, there is the potential for complacency and a repeat occurrence.

On behalf of the Agua Hedionda Lagoon Foundation, Eric asked me to serve as its spokesperson, in order to recognize the local community for its successful eradication effort, and to place in context its worldwide significance. Also, I wanted to raise/sustain awareness of the ongoing Killer Algae threat. I remained the spokesperson through 2014.

The lesson learned is that the Carlsbad lagoons, and all lagoons in and around population centers, can no longer be left alone to self-sustain; they now need human stewardship to remain healthy. *Caulerpa taxifolia* is only one of the many potential introductions or accumulations that need to be avoided to maintain a vibrant ecosystem. Their avoidance is dependent on human monitoring and oversight. As with any maintenance program, this is mostly predictable and needs to be budgeted. Maintenance cannot be neglected without predictably dire consequences.

It was a privilege to work to benefit the Lagoon Foundation, and an honor to be deemed worthy and invited in by Eric. He and I are now old friends, as I'm certain I've known him in other lifetimes. Mr. Muñoz is a special person. There is no better storyteller on earth. I would follow Eric if he asked, without the need to know where. His stories would be reason enough to follow, but his purity of heart and earth-bound soul ensure that whatever his cause, it is as fine a cause as one could be associated with. The only thing Eric likes better than people is being on, in, or near water. If it floats, he's ridden it. If it swims, he swam with it. Part fish, part shaman, protector of the sea, friend to all. Not long after meeting, I took to calling him by the name of one of my favorite childhood superheroes, Aquaman.

Southern California is the only place on the planet that has seen the eradication of *Caulerpa taxifolia*. It also happens to be where Eric Noel Muñoz, the real-life Aquaman, lives and plays. The killer algae may have been a worthy opponent, but against Aquaman it didn't stand a chance.

Christopher Knight • Los Angeles, California
April 2016

CHRISTOPHER KNIGHT starred in the popular TV series *The Brady Bunch*. He has been an environmental and ocean advocate in Southern California for many years.

Preface
Alexandre Meinesz, Author, *Killer Algae*

In the spring of 2000, I was invited to Washington, DC, by US government agencies to explain the problem posed by *Caulerpa taxifolia* in the Mediterranean. Professors well known for their research on terrestrial invasive species attended the meeting. A key question was whether to ban the sale of *Caulerpa* to aquarium enthusiasts in the United States.

The day after my return to Nice I received an email from Rachel Woodfield, a biologist from San Diego, California, with a photograph of an alga, asking me if I recognized it. Not only was it obviously *Caulerpa taxifolia*, but I saw immediately that its robust morphology identified it as the invasive strain from the Mediterranean. It had just been found at Agua Hedionda, a lagoon north of San Diego! It took only two months for lab scientists who had spent two years studying the genetics of different strains of *Caulerpa taxifolia* to confirm that it was indeed the Mediterranean strain that had just been found in California. The article on the genetics of *Caulerpa taxifolia* appeared in *Nature* in August 2000 with the title "Invasive Alga Reaches California."

In 2002 I was invited to San Diego by a task force, the Southern California *Caulerpa* Action Team (SCCAT), for a conference on the possibility of eradicating the algae at Agua Hedionda and in Huntington Harbour, Orange County, where it had just been found. At San Diego, in addition to hearing many scientific reports on *Caulerpa taxifolia*, I learned that Agua Hedionda Lagoon had been mapped in minute detail by divers from an environmental consulting firm in order to understand the extent of the *Caulerpa taxifolia* invasion. More than 1,000 square meters were covered, but with widely scattered individuals.

Of the 100 participants at the conference, only three of us knew the *Caulerpa taxifolia* situation in the Mediterranean well: my student Thierry Thibaut, a diving colleague from a Croatian university (Ante Zuljevic) who had explored sites invaded by the algae on his country's Adriatic coast, and me.

I was astounded by the outcome of this meeting. After the scientific lectures, the three people with knowledge of the Mediterranean invasion found themselves in a workshop that was very unusual for us Europeans. A facilitator, who had no biological training, led the workshop. The chosen participants were local university types, personnel of the environmental consulting firm who had mapped the invasion in Agua Hedionda, representatives of the local government agencies in charge of environmental matters, and a good number of lab biologists who were certainly not divers but who knew the genetics of the algae. Among these latter were European biologists who had been commissioned by the French Academy of Sciences to study *Caulerpa* genetics. I knew that the Oceanographic Museum of Monaco was affiliated with a French foundation managed by members of the French Academy of Sciences; thus I was not overjoyed to see these European biologists at the workshop. Furthermore, their work had recently been superseded by research of a team of geneticists I had managed to assemble. Without any government help we had been able to come up with funding from our own laboratories to study and publish the article on *Caulerpa* genetics in *Nature*. The European geneticists (financed indirectly by Monaco) who had lost the race to publication on *Caulerpa* genetics always seemed to me to be resolutely hostile.

It was then that the facilitator raised the issue of eradication, asking the chosen participants for answers to some simple questions. In particular, we were asked to summarize our views on the probability of success of an eradication attempt. Thierry, Ante, and I were the only ones who were enthusiastic about the idea. Knowing the details of the biology of the algae in the field, and as all three of us were certified professional divers, we were convinced that it was imperative to attempt the eradication, which we deemed to have a 90% probability of success. But most of the participants were against the idea, and the European geneticists estimated the chances of success at only 30%. Thierry, Ante, and I struggled to make it apparent that our opinion was more relevant than that of lab biologists.

We never learned who made the decision to go ahead with the attempt and what arguments proved decisive, but I believe our vigorous efforts were the determining factor.

Unfortunately, I was unable to remain in San Diego, because the conference was held smack in the middle of my teaching assignments in Nice. I regret never having gotten to see Agua Hedionda Lagoon, where the algae had established itself.

But the members of the team that eradicated the algae at Agua Hedionda, including Eric Muñoz, regularly kept me abreast of developments during the eradication project and on the enormous amount of work to find the scattered *Caulerpa* individuals that appeared for a few years following the operation. The rope-guided dives in murky waters with the goal of examining every square inch of the bottom were absolutely fundamental to the success. The least little individual of *Caulerpa* that was missed could lead eventually to a new proliferation. The divers did their work well. After several years of monitoring, the evidence was clear: the project had succeeded!

This was, to my knowledge, the first time anywhere in the world in which an invasive marine species had been definitively eradicated.

Therefore, the "memoir" by one of the main protagonists of this unusual saga is well worth publication. This history has certainly left its mark on Eric Muñoz, and I will always remember him from the time, in autumn 2015, when I took him (in his swim suit) into refreshing waters and a sea somewhat stirred up by a recent storm in search of the "killer algae" at Cap Ferrat near my home. Although the algae had greatly regressed by then for reasons that are still unclear, I found a good sample that I dragged up from the seafloor and presented to Eric. He was like a little boy who'd just gotten a Christmas gift! He had come in pilgrimage to the shores where it had all begun. He could see the very object that had preoccupied so many people, and he could recall the joy he felt at having successfully stopped its invasion in his own homeland.

It is above all the quick response and the exemplary organization of the divers who monitored the invaded zone that allowed this operation to succeed. I raise a well-deserved salute to all those who contributed to this project!

Alexandre Meinesz • Nice, France
April 2016

Introduction

The World According to Invasive Species

This story involves a tragedy that is mapping itself around the world—the sad reality of invasive species threatening natural environments and coastal areas. Ecosystems hang in dynamic balance, depending upon particular geographical and other biophysical factors. However, global hot spots are expanding, impacting, and in some cases, significantly displacing native plants and animals. Blame lies with the introduction of biological species to new habitats and locations, as well as the development and diffusion of genetic clones of biological species. One example is the bottom-growing marine seaweed known as *Caulerpa taxifolia*, the "Killer Algae."

This story is my account of the first known eradication of *Caulerpa taxifolia* worldwide. It occurred in Agua Hedionda Lagoon, a coastal estuary in Carlsbad, a beach community located 30 miles north of San Diego, California. It involved a six-year campaign from initial detection in mid-2000 to declaration of formal eradication by the California Department of Fish and Game in July 2006. The community experience of this precedent-setting success, and the continued global urgency and relevance of the lessons learned, serves as the basis for this story. It also involves a fundamental player: human nature. The impacts of human action, and the grave consequences of human inaction, are daunting. Gaining community consensus and pursuing scientifically sound policies make perfect sense until it has to be executed in real life.

This story is also a tribute to the vision and power of many individuals, whose intelligence and passion should inspire communities worldwide to sustain natural ecosystems by maintaining focus on invasive species. Legacies have already been established, and continue to be, by those on the leading edge of this effort.

What is *Caulerpa taxifolia*?

In tropical ocean waters and latitudes, the bottom-growing *Caulerpa taxifolia* seaweed occurs naturally. Correspondingly, growth is kept in check because the native ecosystem supports other species that can feed on it. In Europe during the 1970s, an invasive strain of this seaweed, which represented a genetic clone that revealed rapid growth qualities that needed minimum maintenance, was observed.

Because of this, and its beautiful appearance, rapid growth, and cold water tolerance, the Mediterranean strain of *Caulerpa taxifolia* became hugely popular for the aquarium trade, both in home use and institutional, large-scale aquariums. Ultimately, in 1984, the Monaco Oceanographic Museum made an aquarium release of the seaweed into ocean waters. The "aquarium" seaweed established in local waters, and then spread to other areas of the adjacent French Riviera coastline via the unknowing aid of fishing, boating, and anchoring activities. The spread was due to the reproductive qualities of *Caulerpa taxifolia*, which involves fragmentation. One small fragment alone could detach from the main plant, float away, and colonize a new area. *Caulerpa taxifolia* soon covered coral reef and sandy coastal ecosystems to unprecedented magnitudes in portions of the Mediterranean Sea.

It took some time before we learned the human role in the origin and diffusion of the "fake" seaweed. The introduced *Caulerpa taxifolia* clone can grow in colder waters than its natural tropical cousin. Since fish do not eat it, the lack of predators allows unrestricted growth. These attributes warrant concern on a global level, since they represent ecosystem threats including the Mediterranean Sea, the Australian coastlines of South Australia and New South Wales, and Southern California.

During June 2000, the first known Western Hemisphere detection of the aquarium strain of *Caulerpa taxifolia* occurred in Agua Hedionda Lagoon. It was shocking news. The source of the infestation is tied to the release of home aquarium contents. Through a curbside release, or a release directly into an adjacent storm drain, *Caulerpa taxifolia* fragments ended up in the lagoon waters and then became established on the sandy bottom. The stage was set for its eventual spread. Most concerning was that fragments could be carried out of the lagoon through the ocean inlet by outgoing tidal currents, and then establish a presence on the adjacent shoreline, coastal reefs, or offshore kelp beds. An unprecedented response was generated from local, regional, state, and federal players with international interface, collaboration, and inspiration.

At the same time, infestation was detected at another Southern California location: the private yacht basins and waterways of Huntington Harbour, in north Orange County just south of Long Beach. Unlike Agua Hedionda Lagoon, there is no short and direct open-ocean connection with the Harbour waters, which are lined with lovely homes and yacht slips. Tidal flows circulate through lengthy and circuitous channel ways, adding an element of control to the site, compared to a direct open-ocean outlet. Nevertheless, survey and eradication efforts were diligently applied to Huntington Harbour as a parallel effort to the Carlsbad site. The Huntington Harbour situation was due to the same vector of infestation: the release of home aquarium contents directly into the waters adjacent to residences.

With two locations infested with the invasive aquarium strain of *Caulerpa taxifolia* in Southern California, this story will focus on the Carlsbad situation, given my direct involvement and the concern of the open-ocean connection presented by Agua Hedionda Lagoon.

As a senior planner in the Carlsbad Planning Department involved with coastal zone management, I became the designated liaison between city management, city staff, the community, and the multi-agency team SCCAT (Southern California *Caulerpa* Action Team), which was formed to combat the seaweed from 2000 through mid-2006.

While declared "eradicated" in July 2006, *Caulerpa taxifolia* could conceivably get reintroduced. The issue of baseline and periodic monitoring over time also applies to other wetlands along the Southern California coastline, and elsewhere in the world. Thus, it warrants long-term monitoring.

This story is not a technical manual on the specifics of the eradication technique carried out by consulting scientists and resource agency staff. Rather, it is intended to convey our community's raw experience to address the challenges of this serious threat. After all, we had no previous examples worldwide of a successful eradication of *Caulerpa taxifolia* to follow.

This whole experience remains a personal and professional highlight for me in many ways. Given the apparent randomness with which *Caulerpa taxifolia* appeared in one of Carlsbad's three lagoons, let alone the Southern California coastline, it would be grossly negligent on my part to ignore this fateful opportunity to outline my perspective on how this unfolded. Hopefully, the lessons learned and patterns revealed will provide global value regarding the awareness of *Caulerpa taxifolia*, the need for sustainable coastal resource stewardship, the benefits of learning from the experiences of others, invasive species in general, and the consequences of a mutant genetic clone being unleashed in coastal ecosystems.

Addressing the Most Serious Coastal Issues

Among the coastal issues facing our generation today, and setting the stage for the marine resource challenges of future generations, the most serious demand immediate attention from the realms of science, policy, funding, and changes in human behavior. In my worldview, these "most serious" issues include global climate change and corresponding sea level rise, overfishing, marine debris, sewage and toxic chemicals in our oceans, and invasive species.

In *A Sustainable Future for the Mediterranean* (Guillaume Benoit & Aline Comeau, 2005) the worldwide realization of the damage of invasive species to native ecosystems is clearly stated on page 326 in a chapter that includes an overview of the *Caulerpa* invasion: "On a global scale, invading species are the second most important cause of biodiversity loss, after physical destruction of habitats. Introducing species from afar is a particular risk because of the absence of natural predators and competitors. The Mediterranean is particularly affected with its nearly 500 non-indigenous marine species." In addition, while addressing the degradation of coastal habitats and species it notes that the Mediterranean is considered to be one of the world's most threatened seas.

Many vectors of transport and introduction can cause invasive species to be located in unintended areas. From the ancient times of rats hitching rides on trans-Pacific Polynesian outriggers, trade routes between the European continent and the Far East, to the pigs on Captain Cook's boats to the South Pacific and the cargo following in the wake of Columbus's journeys to the New World, the transplanting of exotic plants and trans-oceanic movements of livestock and animals provide examples of biological invasions that exist across the planet. For example, a ceremonial release of Asian fish in the northeastern US, tied to religious practices and cultural beliefs, can help explain the invasive snakehead phenomenon. This strange non-native fish can essentially crawl on land and live out of the water for days. It thrives in places like New York's Central Park Lake, where it has no natural predators.

Ocean-going ships, and their intake and release of ballast water along oceanic shipping routes that span the globe, serves up another common vector of invasive species movements. Transportation of soil and plants containing the Coqui frog native to the Caribbean island of Puerto Rico, and subsequent transplanting in upscale residential gardens in Hawaii, have triggered an unstoppable frog invasion there. A fundamental lesson and pattern? Humans are central to the invasive species equation.

However, some methods of invasive species transport are beyond the control of man's actions. Look at the March 2011 tsunami event in Japan. The powerful ocean-going back surges of the tsunami waves pulled a variety of shoreline structures and marine life offshore and into the clockwise rotation of the North Pacific gyre. Over two years later, the first landfall of tsunami debris arrived on the North American West Coast, due to currents controlling gyre movement. Attached to these floating objects were marine organisms that originated in Japan, now carried onto the West Coast. Thus, sometimes the movement of invasive species cannot be controlled: they are put into motion by forces of nature outside the ability of humans to alter, divert, or abate.

Indeed, reading about invasive species provides an uncomfortable combination of science fiction imagination and modern reality:

Weed Threatens Mega-Marina | July 11, 2007

"Named by the Global Invasive Species Specialist Group as among the 100 worst invasive alien species threatening biodiversity, *Caulerpa taxifolia*'s presence in areas adjacent to millionaire developer Denis O'Neil's marina proposal has Woollahra councilor David Shoebridge concerned."
http://www.dailytelegraph.com.au/news/nsw/weed-threatens-mega-marina/story-e6freuzi-1111113928357

Mutant Seaweed Invades Marina | May 7, 2008

"A mutant seaweed that threatens South Australia's $500 million a year fishing and aquaculture industries has been found in Adelaide marina."
http://www.adelaidenow.com.au/news/south-australia/mutant-seaweed-invades-marina/story-e6frea83-1111116281976

Noxious Weed a Threat to Fishing | August 1, 2009

"A noxious weed that could threaten fish stocks has been left unchecked to infest NSW (New South Wales, Australia) waters. And now the State Government has admitted that the invasion by *Caulerpa taxifolia*—originally an aquarium weed—is so bad it will never be eradicated."
http://www.heraldsun.com.au/news/noxious-weed-a-threat-to-fishing/story-e6frf7jo-1225756922793

Invasive Predator Fish That Can Live Outside Water Hunted in Central Park
April 30, 2013

"The snakehead species, native to Asia and Russia, has no natural predators and is illegal in most US states. But federal agents have uncovered illegal snakehead selling operations in several states, including New York, Texas, Florida, and Missouri. And the so-called "Frankenfish" was recently spotted in the Central Park lake, leading environmental officials to order the survey."

https://www.yahoo.com/news/blogs/sideshow/snakehead-fish-central-park-125950046.html?ref=gs

Tiny Coqui Frog Becomes a Big Problem in Hawaii | December 27, 2014

"In Puerto Rico, the coqui's call is likened to sweet music and is celebrated in poetry, literature, and song. But to the Hawaii Invasive Species Council, a state agency, their vast numbers create a "loud, incessant and annoying call from dusk to dawn." The male frogs chirp at about 90 decibels, roughly as loud as a lawn mower or garbage disposal. The density of coquis in the Aloha State is three times greater than in Puerto Rico. There are so many frogs that larger ones have taken to eating smaller ones, although cannibalism won't be enough to keep their numbers in check."

http://www.latimes.com/nation/la-na-coqui-frog-hawaii-20141228-story.html

How These 3,000-Plus Invasive Goldfish Are Threatening a Whole Colorado Lake Ecosystem | April 7, 2015

"Colorado wildlife officials say they believe someone dumped four to five pet goldfish in a Boulder lake about two years ago, and they have now multiplied to over 3,000 to 4,000 fish."

https://gma.yahoo.com/3-000-plus-invasive-goldfish-threatening-whole-colorado-152609378--abc-news-pets.html

Fish Found in Suspected Tsunami Debris Boat Quarantined | April 17, 2015

"The wreckage of a fishing boat that appears to be debris from the 2011 Japanese tsunami was carrying some unexpected passengers—fish from Japanese waters—when it was spotted off the Oregon coast. Finding live fish in tsunami debris is significant because scientists previously predicted that live organisms would not drift across the ocean on floating objects."

https://www.yahoo.com/news/fish-found-suspected-tsunami-debris-boat-quarantined-193833925.html?ref=gs

Invasive Lionfish Discovered in Brazil | April 27, 2015

"Lionfish have overwhelmed ecosystems in the Gulf of Mexico and the Caribbean over the past three decades, eating or out-competing native species in what has been called the worst marine invasion ever. Now the fish seem to have extended their range to South America."

http://www.nature.com/news/invasive-lionfish-discovered-in-brazil-1.17414

Are Invasive Lionfish Spreading to the Mediterranean? | June 21, 2016

"New sightings of lionfish in the Mediterranean are sparking fears the invasive species could wreak havoc on local economies. The International Union for the Conservation of Nature said in a statement that the group has confirmed sightings of the highly invasive species off the shores of Turkey and Cyprus. In the United States, lionfish were first spotted in Florida in the mid-1980s and have continued to spread rapidly. Florida's Wildlife Commission estimates there are millions of the fish, which have no predators, and damaged native fish and shrimp populations. Florida officials have said the fish may have been released from someone's home aquarium."

http://www.usatoday.com/story/news/nation-now/2016/06/21/invasive-species-lionfish-florida-now-mediterranean-conservation-group/86173800/

Snake in the Grass! Huge Everglades Python Shows Invasive Issue
August 1, 2015

"Burmese pythons are native to Southeast Asia, and only established a foothold in the Florida ecosystem after they were released into the wild by (or escaped from) pet owners and breeders."

https://www.yahoo.com/news/snake-grass-huge-everglades-python-shows-invasive-issue-225922758.html?ref=gs

A Terminator Fish Is Moving at Record Speed Toward the Great Lakes
November, 3, 2015

"Asian carp, which threaten a host of native species, advanced 12 miles toward Lake Michigan in just one month. Asian carp were imported from Southeast Asia to the Southern United States by fish farms. Flooding allowed them to escape into the Mississippi River system, where they migrated into the Missouri and Illinois rivers. Black carp, another Asian species, feed on mollusks, threatening native mussel and sturgeon populations. The carp can also damage property and injure people. Silver carp are startled by

boat motors, causing them to leap up to 10 feet in the air, slamming into vessels and the people on them."
http://www.takepart.com/article/2015/11/03/destructive-carp-are-66-miles-closer-invading-great-lakes

Carp Ravage Australia's Food Bowl | April 14, 2016

"Like the Mississippi River in the US, the tributaries near this farming hub helped open up Australia's interior more than a century ago. Now European carp are devastating the lifeblood of the nation's food bowl. The invasive species now represent 80% of all fish in southern Australia's Murray–Darling river system, up from 58% four years ago, in a region that produces a third of the country's total agricultural output."
http://www.wsj.com/articles/herpes-australias-possible-weapon-to-tackle-a-fishy-problem-1460585506

Invasive Plants Spread Fast in Billion-Dollar Threat: Study | August 19, 2015

"Many of the world's plants are turning "alien," spread by people into new areas where they choke out native vegetation in a worsening trend that causes billions of dollars in damage, scientists said. With continuing globalization and increasing international traffic and trade, it is very likely that more species will be introduced outside their natural range."
http://www.reuters.com/article/us-environment-plants-idUSKCN0Q-O1VU20150819

Aquariums require careful handling and oversight. No matter how large or small an aquarium may be, releasing its contents is something conducted by conscious human action. Adding the specter of a mutant genetic clone into the invasive species equation creates a synergy of problematic management and an accelerated portal to ecosystem imbalance. In fact, many people have told me over the years that their own personal home aquariums were rapidly overwhelmed with the invasive *Caulerpa* seaweed. Like a Frankenstein monster that escapes from the creator's laboratory, and then unknowingly gets cloned and wholly reproduced with every loss of a hair particle, or every clip of a toenail, the ability for *Caulerpa taxifolia* to reproduce from fragmentation is no less daunting. Combined with the real-life evidence of having smothered and impacted coastal and marine ecosystems, from coral reef habitats to rocky substrate and sandy bottom shorelines, the aquarium strain of *Caulerpa taxifolia* challenges the imagination to fully understand and appreciate.

If confronted with this situation, the ensuing result is one of extreme challenge, ending in likely submission or failure. This was the case of the Mediterranean experience, outlined in the 1999 book *Killer Algae* (The University of Chicago Press) by French biologist and researcher Dr. Alexandre Meinesz. A successful control plan requires the elusive combination of human intelligence, partnership, and the capitalization of luck. To combat the monster, there has to be a prudent, technical response absent emotion. Unlike the monster in a dream that eventually succumbs to the waking hours of morning light, we had to face the monster in the bright light of day. It made us battle in a multi-dimensional manner for the resumed health of our coastal lagoon while fearing the Pacific Ocean and our California coastline could be under threat. Surely, losing one coastal lagoon initiates a process of continued loss for marine resources and coastline habitats. For us, *Caulerpa taxifolia* was a real-life science fiction monster that grabbed our hearts, breath, and attention all at once.

Chapter 1
Can You Say *Caulerpa taxifolia?*

Caulerpa taxifolia occurs naturally in tropical waters, kept in check via native fish species that feed on it. However, the invasive version of this seaweed, a cold-water tolerant mutant genetic clone observed and cultivated at Germany's Stuttgart Zoo in the 1970s, was widely used within aquariums over the following decades.

This desirability and popularity extended to the aquarium trade, including institutional aquariums such as the Oceanographic Museum of Monaco. Dr. Alexandre Meinesz, a university marine biology professor in neighboring Nice, France, was also an avid recreational and research scuba diver. In *Killer Algae*, he recounts his firsthand experience with the initial detections of *Caulerpa taxifolia* in the waters fronting the Monaco Aquarium in the mid to late 1980s. He then outlines the profoundly challenging scientific and political dimensions of securing understanding and support to address the grave issues involved with the presence and geographic diffusion of *Caulerpa taxifolia*.

Over time, the lack of governmental and agency support, combined with institutional inaction, created peril for the Mediterranean Sea. Along with it came a contributing issue of political sensitivity: the godfather of marine ecology, Jacques Cousteau, was an aquarium director.

Meinesz and others saw patches of *Caulerpa taxifolia* offshore of the aquarium's outfall pipe. A release of aquarium tank water via the outfall pipe likely caused the source of infestation that triggered the Mediterranean invasion. However, in his book, Meinesz recounts conversations with staff members that aquarium contents were also tossed directly into the sea, including *Caulerpa taxifolia*. Several Mediterranean nations are now affected to varying degrees by this invasive seaweed: Monaco, France, Italy, Spain, Tunisia, Croatia, Malta, Cyprus, and Greece.

The "aquarium" strain genetic clone established itself and spread to other coastal areas in Monaco and adjacent Mediterranean waters. Seaweed fragments attached to diving gear, fishing equipment, and/or anchoring lines invaded new areas once the user returned to the ocean at different locations. Over time, this process advanced *Caulerpa's* dispersal and geographic scope. In addition, ballast water movements likely played a role within harbor areas. Only one centimeter of the seaweed is needed to find sediment and begin a new infestation.

Many years passed before these dynamics and related agents of diffusion were understood, let alone socially accepted.

In addition, the aquarium strain has a higher salinity and light tolerance, and can grow in colder waters compared to its natural tropical counterpart. In general terms, the native *Caulerpa* seaweed found in tropical waters does not have the expanded thermal tolerance of the mutant clone aquarium strain, which can tolerate temperatures of 46 to 86 degrees Fahrenheit. This translates to several degrees of coastline latitude now susceptible to *Caulerpa taxifolia*. For example, more than 500 miles of California coastline, from the Mexican border to San Francisco Bay, could be invaded by the aquarium strain, compared to the limited warm water range of the native tropical strain.

On a larger scale, when considering the role of kelp in oxygen production, the protection of natural kelp coastlines and related ecosystems worldwide is an obvious objective. *Caulerpa taxifolia*, especially when combined with impacts from other invasive species and ocean pollution, creates a current global threat. Public awareness and proper aquarium use, in addition to appropriate laws, need full and rapid effectiveness.

Infestations of *Caulerpa taxifolia* also are occurring in southeastern Australian wetlands. The first infestation hit the South Australia coastal city of Adelaide in 2002. Sydney Harbour has been contending with *Caulerpa* since the early 2000s, along with several other New South Wales wetlands.

Laying the Foundation in Carlsbad

Key individuals and personalities, cloaked with civic, agency, and/or corporate directives and resources, quickly developed a mindset that would lay the foundation to assess and treat our situation. At the time, I was twelve years into a nearly eighteen-year career with the Planning Department staff of the City of Carlsbad. As a senior planner I was involved with coastal planning issues. By late 2000 I began the role of designated liaison between city hall and SCCAT (Southern California *Caulerpa* Action Team), the multi-agency task team assembled to combat the strange seaweed residing in our local beloved lagoon.

Agua Hedionda Lagoon had hosted over 50 years of recreational boating. It provided a community resource for fishing, jet-skiing, water-skiing, wake boarding, and passive vessel use such as sailing, canoeing, and kayaking. Today, you can add stand-up paddleboarding to the list. Agua Hedionda Lagoon represents a strong community value and source of pride (and property values) within Carlsbad and the surrounding region. No other coastal lagoon in San Diego County located between Oceanside Harbor and San Diego Bay allows for in-water recreational use. Those recreational water uses at Agua Hedionda became threatened, along with the biological resources of the lagoon, due to the presence of *Caulerpa taxifolia*. While there was no eradication precedent for us to follow, something impossible to ignore was the potential loss of fishery resources and recreational uses, and the corresponding onset of economic adversity.

Origin of Agua Hedionda Lagoon

In 1769, Spanish explorers and missionaries led by Don Gaspar de Portolá came across a tidal lagoon with decaying fish and a foul odor. Soldiers called the location "stinking waters," and thus the lagoon's name: Agua Hedionda.

Agua Hedionda Lagoon is the coastal endpoint of an extensive watershed that extends for miles inland with a diverse range of ecosystems and habitats including Lake Calavera and Calavera Mountain. Watershed drainage culminates in the confluence of the Calavera and Agua Hedionda Creeks entering the eastern edge of the lagoon. The current configuration of the Agua Hedionda Lagoon waterbody was created in 1954, dredged from existing wetlands into the 388-acre water body that exists today. The slough-like wetlands were transformed into the deeper lagoon basins that now circulate daily with ocean tidal flow, designed to accommodate the construction and operation of a regional power generating facility (Encina Power Station). The resulting tidal prism facilitates the passage of ocean water to be used for cooling the power plant turbines that generate electricity. Since power plant operations rely on ocean water flowing through the lagoon, maintenance dredging is necessary to remove inland, watershed-sourced sediment, as well as accumulated littoral beach sand entering the lagoon inlet from the ocean and adjacent shoreline.

As part of the environmental mitigation imposed by affected resource agencies to allow for these dredging operations, the power plant was required to plant, establish, and maintain native eelgrass along the bottom of the lagoon. Consulting biologists Merkel & Associates of San Diego were employed to monitor (via scuba diving) the eelgrass growth over several subsequent years.

The native eelgrass provides essential bottom habitat, so that the lagoon can function as a biological nursery for marine resources. It also stabilizes the lagoon bottom to reduce scouring during extreme tidal conditions. During a routine eelgrass-monitoring dive in June 2000, Merkel staff biologist Rachel Woodfield and her dive team, including Steve Rink, first detected *Caulerpa*.

Part of the challenge in garnering public concern is that *Caulerpa taxifolia* is not located on the water's surface. It is bottom-growing, and thus, "invisible." By the time an economic impact is felt (loss of fish habitat, tourism, water use), the time for an environmental solution may be long gone. Naively or otherwise, Carlsbad was hoping against all odds for a different outcome.

The release of aquarium contents and entry into marine waters is how *Caulerpa taxifolia* threatens ecosystems worldwide, including Agua Hedionda Lagoon. The size of the aquarium does not matter. In Carlsbad, a residential street uphill and adjacent to the north shore of the lagoon (Hoover Street) includes a storm drain, located at its base, which empties directly into lagoon waters. The in-water detection happened near the storm drain outfall. Up the street, curbside rinsing and release of a home aquarium and its contents down the curb, into the storm drain and through the outfall, is the likely source of the Carlsbad infestation.

From this, we learned a fundamental lesson quickly: do not dump or rinse aquarium contents into natural areas or storm drains which will drain to lagoons, wetlands, harbors, or ocean areas.

Coastal Zone Management and Invasive Species

Coastal zone management that promotes sustainability, with prudent public policies based on sound science, is critically needed in our world. Coastal areas need assessment and management on large regional scales. These regional areas need careful attention where they interface. If properly implemented, an effective plan for global ocean preservation can be achieved.

This is the core message of Colin Woodard's book *Ocean's End* (Basic Books, Parseus Books Group). A journalist specializing in global affairs, Woodard chronicles various challenged or damaged coastal areas around the world. His book makes a compelling case for prudent coastal zone management on a global scale, and for its implementation—much sooner than later. One main point covered in this lesson-filled book is the dangerous specter of invasive species.

I received this book as a Christmas gift in 1999, and promptly read it front to back. Later in 2000, after the initial detection of *Caulerpa taxifolia* in

Agua Hedionda Lagoon, I read Meinesz's *Killer Algae*. Stunned by the ominous threat posed by this seaweed, I flashed back to *Ocean's End*. On page 25, I found the overview of *Caulerpa taxifolia* with a succinctly delivered story of its threat and damage to the Mediterranean and the coastlines of France, Monaco, Italy, Sicily, Majorca, and Croatia. For me, it clearly achieved prophetic proportions. *Ocean's End* also introduced and profiled Meinesz. I was hugely inspired and awestruck by his overview, in which he delivered the knockout summary sentence regarding the status of *Caulerpa taxifolia* worldwide: "Man can do nothing. Nobody can stop it."

Reading *Killer Algae* made me feel sad for our local lagoon. Northern San Diego County is blessed with a series of coastal lagoons. Running south to north, and beginning about ten miles north of San Diego, they include Los Peñasquitos, San Dieguito, San Elijo, Batiquitos, Agua Hedionda, and Buena Vista Lagoons. A string of biodiversity hot spots and wetland pearls, our lagoons are natural treasures within their communities. I was sad that something like *Caulerpa taxifolia* could exist in our backyard. I thought about those Mediterranean coastlines, where an ecosystem conversion could occur at a scale that would challenge human intelligence to understand.

Killer Algae also opened my eyes to what our community truly faced. I realized with a somber uneasiness that it would be a challenge to get our city and community to realize the gravity of *Caulerpa's* presence. This was an easy conclusion, given the amazing challenges that Meinesz and the scientific community faced in persuading officials in the Mediterranean to seriously address their growing dilemma. The institutional and political obstacles that emerged only served to further the problem over time while eroding feasible options for successful and timely eradication. In fact, the human nature aspect of his story is quite troubling. Despite compelling scientific arguments regarding the growth and threat of *Caulerpa* throughout regional stretches of cross-national Mediterranean coastal areas, adequate policy and funding responses did not occur to a significantly effective degree. My "take-home" message was to assist the scientific and agency response led by SCCAT to effectively interface with the Carlsbad leaders and community. Only a collective and collaborative vision of complete eradication success could fuel a true partnership among the varied stakeholders in place at Agua Hedionda Lagoon.

After the initial detection and verification of *Caulerpa taxifolia* in June 2000, a variety of agencies, entities, and stakeholders became engaged in understanding the problem so an effective response could be mounted. SCCAT played the lead role.

As noted earlier, another infestation was detected about 60 miles north of Carlsbad, within Huntington Harbour. Since Huntington Harbour is a residential yacht harbor setting, clearly the source of release was a home or deck aquarium. Some aquariums there even draw direct harbor seawater for use. Both Carlsbad and Huntington Harbour were targets of SCCAT efforts to eradicate *Caulerpa taxifolia*. Likewise, both sites enjoyed the victory of eradication in July 2006.

This story outlines the Carlsbad experience in a chronological manner from 1998 to late 2015. It begins with an introduction of key players, affected stakeholders, and an overview of the biological context of *Caulerpa taxifolia*.

Chapter 2
Agencies and Entities: Who's at the Table?

SCCAT: Multi-Agency Coalition

Depending on one's perspective and experience, the California coastline is either blessed or cursed with various overlays of regulatory control and environmental oversight. In either case, regulatory effectiveness can often come down to the individual will of the agency staff member involved and/or the related agency's financial budget. While short on funds (no agency budgets had allocations for a biological invasion such as *Caulerpa*), there was no shortage of agencies involved. In particular, four agencies formed the core of SCCAT: The Regional Water Quality Control Board of San Diego and Orange Counties (RWQCB); US Department of Agriculture (USDA); National Marine Fisheries Service (NMFS); and the California Department of Fish and Game (CDFG).

The RWQCB had a staff member of incredible vision and integrity. Greig Peters was a serious advocate of his agency's role to monitor and enforce water quality in the coastal watersheds of San Diego County. I had the benefit of interfacing with him while staffing a joint powers committee for Buena Vista Lagoon, north of Agua Hedionda. This joint powers committee held an advisory role, with staff and elected officials participating from the cities upstream and adjacent to the lagoon.

In addition, area stakeholders and affected resource agency staff attended our Buena Vista committee meetings. It was then that I first saw Peters in action. He provided the calm, convincing voice from the back of the room that politely but properly made salient points for lagoon stewardship relative to water quality control and existing regulations. He wove logic between the scientific context, policy options, and funding opportunities. Seen by all as a credible and effective public agency staff member, he was respected across the board.

Therefore, when he became involved with the *Caulerpa taxifolia* situation in Agua Hedionda Lagoon, he was the first to speak and act in no uncertain terms. The presence of the invasive seaweed in our coastal lagoon required immediate and effective action. To lose this challenge would equate to the loss of native coastal habitat in Agua Hedionda and beyond. He took the lead to streamline response processes. Many attribute the eventual success of *Caulerpa*'s eradication to his early and vigorous inspiration to act swiftly, with a sense of urgency. (Unfortunately, health issues claimed the life of this California coastline champion in 2002.)

As SCCAT formed, a successor from within the San Diego County RWQCB staff, Bruce Posthumus, was designated as the agency representative in addition to supporting staff member Chiara Clemente. He was named SCCAT chair. Bruce's leadership in various coastal San Diego County watershed efforts was likewise characterized by calm effectiveness. This style proved to be invaluable as he began to steer SCCAT through very uncharted waters.

Because invasive species can affect agricultural production and eventually food supply, the United States Department of Agriculture (USDA) became involved. This federal agency has extensive experience in treating freshwater invasive species and implementing eradication programs. However, this saltwater invader introduced new scenarios and situations that represented unique challenges. Nevertheless, the experience of the USDA, including research and academic resources based at University of California, Davis, near Sacramento, provided additional key players. This included Dr. Lars Anderson, known internationally for various efforts regarding aquatic invasions. As a member of SCCAT, Anderson represented the USDA. Also representing UC Davis and acting as resources for SCCAT were Dr. Ted Grosholz and Dr. Susan Williams, who came to the team by way of the Bodega Bay Marine Laboratory. She would play an important role regarding legislation affecting the sale, transport, and possession of *Caulerpa*.

Another federal agency, the National Marine Fisheries Service, came aboard under the auspices of NOAA (National Oceanic and Atmospheric Administration). Given the impact to fishery resources and related biological impacts to the coastal zone, this agency was one of four core agencies that comprised SCCAT. The NMFS was represented by Bob Hoffman, who served on SCCAT as another highly credible agency staff member. He was also an avid scuba diver.

The California Department of Fish and Game (now renamed the California Department of Fish and Wildlife) was the statewide agency involved with SCCAT. It controls a large ecological preserve in the wetlands adjacent to Agua Hedionda Lagoon. CDFG has a highly vested interest in the immediate area, as well as property ownership and stewardship roles for adjacent San Diego

County coastal lagoons. Staff member Bill Paznokas represented the agency. Another important role that emerged for this agency was the creation of an Invasive Species Coordinator, undertaken by Susan Ellis.

Therefore, the core agencies that comprised SCCAT (RWQCB, USDA, NMFS, and CDFG) provided key staff members and agency resources that laid the foundation for a high-performing team. With this core in place, other stakeholders provided coverage for all the angles that would become identified and made part of the assessment and response effort.

The immediate creation and mobilization of SCCAT was essential to ac-celerate the *Caulerpa* survey efforts and eradication response, which allowed for the elusive "rapid response" that ensued.

Stakeholder Overview

Owners of the Lagoon—The Encinas Power Plant

Cabrillo Power operated the power plant and controlled ownership of the la-goon (subsequently NRG Power). The power plant was represented by legal counsel David Lloyd, who also served on the Agua Hedionda Lagoon Foun-dation board of directors. David's intelligence and profound sense of environ-mental stewardship resulted in diligent action by the power plant that will remain as one of this story's most under-acknowledged elements. The private ownership of the lagoon dates back to 1954. This is in contrast to the public agency ownership that exists for other San Diego County wetlands, including the other two Carlsbad lagoons (Batiquitos and Buena Vista). Tim Heming, George Piantka, and Sheila Henika were also involved as power plant staff, in addition to Michael Pearson who served on the lagoon foundation.

In December 2015, the Claude "Bud" Lewis Carlsbad Desalination Plant opened on the power plant property, and also uses the ocean/lagoon seawater to produce 50 million gallons of potable water daily. Therefore, the desalination plant (largest in the US) is another major stakeholder that benefits from the eradication of *Caulerpa taxifolia*.

Aside from the power plant and desalination facility, a variety of land uses surround the lagoon perimeter: commercial aquaculture, white seabass fish hatchery, YMCA youth camp, residential homes and condos, trails, open space, a California Department of Fish and Wildlife ecological preserve, commercial boating and water sports rental facility, the lagoon foundation's nature center, and agricultural fields.

Local Lagoon Foundation—Agua Hedionda Lagoon Foundation

Agua Hedionda Lagoon has a long history of generational boating use within the community and region. In addition to enjoying international notoriety as the birthplace and early development of wakeboarding, the lagoon also supports water skiing, sailing, boating, stand-up paddling, kayaking, canoeing, and fishing. Agua Hedionda represents an enduring, aesthetic community value, to the point where the open space land use considerations for the expansive south shore in 2006 generated a city council–appointed citizens committee, for which I served as chair. The committee developed successful land use ballot measures that year.

In partnership with SCCAT, the Agua Hedionda Lagoon Foundation (AHLF) emerged into a vital role as a nonprofit organization that could receive and administer critical grants from agency funding sources to pay for eradication activities. Key initial players include Bob Richards, past AHLF President and 2003 Carlsbad Citizen of the Year, and Craig Elliott, a retired aerospace engineer and AHLF member who performed the heroic task of administering complex agency grants and maintaining financial accountability on behalf of SCCAT.

Biologists/Consultants—Merkel & Associates, San Diego

When I was on the city's planning staff, Keith Merkel's reputation was well known as an expert on local lagoon systems from a biological resource assessment and management standpoint. His company, Merkel & Associates (M&A), was already engaged with eelgrass monitoring and revegetation for the power plant within the lagoon. M&A went on to secure subsequent work contracts for mapping, monitoring, eradication, research, and reporting efforts. The innovative thinking, technical command, and raw intelligence of M&A provided great value, showcased by their role in the development of the underwater tarp eradication technique. Key players include Merkel, Rachel Woodfield, Dr. Robert Mooney, and their entire dive team who became the working heroes of this story.

Other Affected Stakeholders—Various

One critically positioned and affected stakeholder was California Watersports, owned at the time by Greg Rusing. California Watersports operates stand-up paddle, kayak, canoe, wakeboard, water ski, jet ski, and boat rentals, as well as classes and related activities. This commercial business is located adjacent to the initial area of *Caulerpa* infestation, underneath the suspect Hoover Street storm drain outfall pipe. The business was significantly affected during the eradication efforts, due to short-term limitations on recreational use. Today, California Watersports operates under the ownership and management of Josh Cantor and his team. Josh has emerged as a valued promoter of lagoon health and recreational use. They no longer have to worry about *Caulerpa taxifolia*, assuming it is not reintroduced into the lagoon.

Other stakeholders included numerous residential property and condominium owners with a collective interest in maintaining recreational uses and corresponding property values. Bristol Cove, with boat docks and its own vessel channel, sits adjacent to the lagoon's north shore. Huge interest was generated in preventing lagoon closures or creating long-term boating limitations. The Bristol Cove Property Owners Association became an effective voice to represent residential and recreational interests.

Independent consulting biologist Steve LePage was also very involved in our effort, serving as well on the SCCAT Scientific Technical Board. In addition, the Carlsbad Boat Club, owned by Jim Courtney and Mike Pfankuch, hosted their location on the north shore of the lagoon to assist with eradication efforts by providing a waterfront staging area. Fishing, academia, and lagoon preservation interests were also active as affected stakeholders.

Hosting City—Carlsbad, California

With just over six miles of open ocean coastline, the city of Carlsbad is about 42 square miles in size. The 2015 population was just under 115,000. Geographically, the city is south of Oceanside and north of Encinitas in San Diego county, and accommodates a pleasing landscape with eastern views of the backcountry, westward ocean horizon vistas, and three coastal lagoons. Key players in 2000 included Mayor Claude "Bud" Lewis; City Council members Ann Kulchin, Matt Hall, Mark Packard, and Norine Sigafoose; City Manager Ray Patchett; City Attorney Ron Ball; Planning Director Michael Holzmiller; Principal Planner Don Rideout, my direct supervisor; and myself.

Brief Biology Background

To gain proper context for understanding the gravity of the impacts from *Caulerpa taxifolia*'s ability to impact native seagrass beds, I share the following background. *Caulerpa* is a genus of green algae known for its single-cell structure. *Caulerpa taxifolia* is one of several species; others include *Caulerpa racemosa* and *Caulerpa mexicana*. *Caulerpa taxifolia* has a long stem, or stolon, from which green leaf-like fronds give a plant-like appearance. The seaweed can become attached to the ocean floor, sandy lagoon bottom, or reef substrate via fine hairs called rhizoids.

The stems, or stolons, have an appearance of creeping along the ocean floor, expanding into new territory. This was the basis for French naturalist Jean Vincent Felix Lamouroux's decision to name the genus *Caulerpa* in 1802, by combining the Greek words for *caulos* (stem) and *erpo* (to creep). The leaves, or fronds (*folia* in Latin), resemble the branches of a conifer (*taxus* in Latin), thus the name: *Caulerpa taxifolia*.

The first problem is fragmentation. The algae can detach and find sediment and initiate colonies of new growth with individual particles down to one centimeter in size. This explains how anchor and fishing lines, scuba diving gear, and similar items act as agents of diffusion, whereby they expand *Caulerpa taxifolia*'s geographic scope as the recreational user reenters the ocean at various locations, or fragmented pieces float away to new areas. Commercial fishing tackle and bottom-dragging lines can further mobilize and spread the algae, in addition to ballast water intake and discharges associated with commercial shipping activities. Sexual reproduction has not been observed in the *Caulerpa taxifolia* clone introduced into the Mediterranean. It lacks the combination of female and male gametes found in the natural strain.

It is important to remember that native *Caulerpa taxifolia* grows without drama in tropical waters and lagoons, such as Lord Howe Island between Australia and New Zealand, and other portions of the South Pacific, Caribbean, eastern Atlantic, and Indian Ocean. It is the genetically distinct clone, which is the "killer algae."

By 1998, it was biologically confirmed that the "aquarium" strain (the clone seaweed) was indeed the "Mediterranean" strain. Its future release from public and private aquariums into marine environments worldwide is a current and pending challenge that threatens coastal areas. The aquarium strain has no natural predators and secretes toxins that do not affect humans, but do impact mollusks, herbivore fish, sea urchins, or submarine flora that would otherwise feed on native *Caulerpa* and keep it in check. It can grow up to three inches per day in pristine waters, as well as in polluted harbors. In the northern hemisphere summer (June through November), it experiences seasonal growth. In the winter and spring, it undergoes a seasonal regression due to cooler waters, but does not completely disappear.

With no natural predators, the Mediterranean strain was poised to proliferate and expand its presence in introduced waters, while displacing native plants and affecting other marine habitats. In one demonstrative and very telling experiment conducted in France, which I have seen on video, a sea urchin is placed in an aquarium with *Caulerpa taxifolia* to see if it will feed on it. Instead, the sea urchin starved itself and then ate its own waste, or even pieces of plastic, rather than the algae. Sea urchins are known to be "generalists" and are very hardy. The fact that they will not eat *Caulerpa taxifolia* truly is significant. Furthermore, the Mediterranean strain is known for being robust and hardy, adapting to a wider range of water quality, light, and temperature conditions, thus exposing more latitude of coastline to threat and invasion. It has the ability to thrive as deeply as 200 to 300 feet in clear water.

Then there is *Zostera*, a genus of common seagrass, native to many sandy shorelines in the US, including Agua Hedionda Lagoon. Found on sandy bottoms in estuaries and coastal wetlands, it aids sediment deposition and erosion control, and also functions as a nursery area for economically important wetland and offshore marine species and shellfish. At Agua Hedionda in 2000, the *Zostera* seagrass and lagoon bottom were in the process of getting invaded by *Caulerpa* when it was detected. A lagoon full of *Caulerpa* would not support the native fishery, thus shutting down fishing and eliminating boating and other active recreational use of the lagoon.

The Mediterranean equivalent to our local eelgrass habitat is the *Posidonia* seagrass meadow, which supports a significant biodiversity of marine life. A huge concern is dealing with the invasive *Caulerpa taxifolia* in the open ocean, where currents and wave action make eradication infeasible. For that reason, a lot of effort was given to lagoon containment, and then the aggressive pursuit of eradication. If played out in this manner, a global first could be achieved.

Chapter 3
1998–2000: Global Alert

Given the Monaco Incident in the mid-1980s and corresponding spread of the invasive aquarium strain, *Caulerpa taxifolia* growth accelerated to unprecedented levels in the Mediterranean Sea between the 1984 and 1998. Coastal ecosystems were at grave risk. The Mediterranean experience had finally reached a critical mass and tipping point whereby global exposure was beginning to occur.

In his book *Killer Algae*, Meinesz outlined various frustrations and obstacles, while the scientific community set about to properly understand this invasive alien. Higher-level governmental and institutional policy decisions did not focus on eradication in early stages, losing valuable time. Meanwhile, genetic research was carried out and predictive distribution modeling of the seaweed advanced. Nevertheless, the scientists were limited by larger political, policy, and funding issues, including inaction to pursue eradication.

What did not limit the Mediterranean science community, or a global science community becoming increasingly and collectively alarmed by *Caulerpa taxifolia*, was the sense of grave urgency. This led to a powerful statement, summarized in letterform by a diverse cartel of concerned scientists and environmental specialists worldwide.

The letter was symbolic, as well as prophetic, sounding the American alarm about the invasive marine seaweed. Dated October 19, 1998, and addressed directly to United States Secretary of the Interior Bruce Babbitt, the letter outlined the dire Mediterranean situation and urged immediate steps to prevent its appearance in American coastal waters. It was signed by over 105 research scientists, ecologists, institutional leaders, and coastal program managers.

Joining Dr. Meinesz in this written warning were entities that truly provided global coverage: the Smithsonian Institution; University of California (UC) Berkeley; UC San Diego; UC Davis; UC Los Angeles; UC Santa Cruz; US Department of Agriculture; Aquatic Plant Control Lab, Florida; Scripps Institute of Oceanography, La Jolla, California; Bishop Museum, Honolulu, Hawaii; Alaska Department of Fish and Game; Hawaii Department of Fish and Game; and universities and institutions in Virginia, Tennessee, Connecticut, New York, Indiana, Colorado, Florida, Pennsylvania, South Carolina, Washington, Massachusetts, Oregon, Arizona, North Carolina, Louisiana, Hawaii, Maryland, and Montana. Countries represented included the US, United Kingdom, France, Australia, Canada, New Zealand, and Brazil.

Clearly, this stunning assemblage of scientific intelligence was making a significantly dramatic statement with its profound foresight and global context. The consensus message left no room for error in interpretation or understanding. It noted the legislative responses to outlaw its transport and sale in France, Spain, and Australia. The letter also reviewed the history of Mediterranean damage. In 1984, *Caulerpa* covered one square yard—3 feet by 3 feet—adjacent to the Monaco Aquarium. By 1989, it covered over two acres in the cove fronting the aquarium. When the letter was written in 1998, the algae had spread to more than 10,000 acres, extending to offshore depths of over 250 feet.

The letter (which can be viewed online at http://www.sfei.org/documents/petition-list-seaweed-caulerpa-taxifolia-prohibited-species-under-federal-noxious-weed-act) went on to specifically identify the threatened American coastal areas if an aquarium-release of *Caulerpa* occurs:

"It is likely only a matter of time before the Mediterranean clone of *Caulerpa taxifolia* is released and becomes established in the United States, threatening coastal waters and coral reefs from North Carolina to Florida and the Gulf of Mexico, and in Southern California, Hawaii, Puerto Rico, the US Virgin Islands, Guam, and Samoa."

In citing the potential damage by eliminating native seagrasses and the corresponding destruction to ecological resources, economic stability, fisheries, diving, and tourism, the letter pointed out how *Caulerpa* can grow rapidly in significant densities, smothering and displacing reef and sandy shore ecosystems by forming ". . . monocultural stands whose impact has been compared to unrolling a carpet of Astroturf across the bottom of the sea."

Finally, what this letter represented was certainly not an emotional or exaggerated plea without scientific evidence or credibility. The lessons of the Mediterranean simply had to pay off somewhere. Promoting global awareness based on the Mediterranean reality was challenging, but attracting preemptive attention and action in another part of the world was truly a hopeful vision.

The Global Alert Is No Hoax

Meanwhile in California, researchers at UC Davis, led by Dr. Edwin Grosholz in collaboration with the Bodega Bay Marine Laboratory and Dr. Susan Williams, along with Maryland's Smithsonian Environmental Research Center, were realizing the gap in research and experience concerning impacts by invasive species in saltwater marine ecosystems. Plenty of research and eradication success exists for aquatic freshwater species; the same level of experience and research did not exist for marine invasive species.

In the May 2000 issue of *Ecology*, a scientific journal published by the Ecological Society of America, an article titled, "The Impacts of a Non-Indigenous Marine Predator in a California Bay," examined the systemic ecological damage rendered by the European green crab, a marine invader. These impacts occurred in their "backyard" of Bodega Bay, adjacent to the Bodega Marine Laboratory. The study considered the emerging realm of introduced species and how they affected multi-trophic level changes to natural coastal environments and marine food webs.

The underlying point in presenting the above information is that there was no benefit of scientific or eradication success when it came to controlling the spread of the aquarium strain of *Caulerpa taxifolia*. The specter of marine invasions was particularly daunting, given the low level of local experience and utter lack of eradication success, or growth containment, in the affected Mediterranean coastal areas.

The Global Alert was no hoax.

During the first half of the 1990s, various committees, research efforts, symposiums, conferences, and workshops were convened and commenced, but no real plan, policy, or action for Mediterranean eradication occurred. Meanwhile, *Caulerpa taxifolia* spread from Monaco and France, to the Balearic Islands off Spain, the Tunisian coast, Italian shorelines, Croatian islands, and locations in the Adriatic Sea. Finally, the Barcelona Declaration in 1995 officially declared *Caulerpa taxifolia* a threat to Mediterranean Sea ecosystems and prioritized its eradication.

Meinesz's book, *Killer Algae*, was actually a translated copy from the original French version, first published in 1997. Dr. Daniel Simberhoff of the University of Tennessee did the translation. Ironically, comprehensive Mediterranean eradication never was mounted. It is generally agreed that eradication was probably infeasible after 1991 due to sheer volume, the ocean depths involved, and overall geographic extent.

The rest of the world took notice—particularly the US. By the year 2000, the global scientific community warning of 1998 had initiated development of national-level planning and public outreach programs. Federal listings on noxious aquatic weed registers were taking place in advance of any actual *Caulerpa taxifolia* detections.

Unless, of course, it was already established and growing in US homeland waters and nobody had yet realized it.

Chapter 4
2000: The Trojan Horse

In June 2000, the quiet discovery that was made in Agua Hedionda Lagoon was part of a multi-year monitoring effort imposed upon the Encina power plant related to dredging. A team of scuba diving marine biologists assessed the health of eelgrass beds along the lagoon bottom. As noted earlier, the power plant was required by resource agency approvals to plant and then monitor the eelgrass after major dredging. Significant dredging is periodically necessary to maintain the tidal prism within the lagoon, so that the flow of ocean water can continue to cool the power plant's energy-producing turbines. If too much sediment builds up along the lagoon bottom or at its ocean inlet, it can lessen the overall tidal flow, which can in turn compromise the ability to cool the energy-generating turbines.

This was a basic design element of power plants constructed in the 1950s along the California coast: to use ocean waters to cool power-generating turbines. The eelgrass stabilizes the sediment along the lagoon bottom so that scouring and erosion from tidal flows can be minimized. A biological function of eelgrass is to provide a food source for the marine resources that use the lagoon as a nursery before transitioning into the offshore coastal waters. This is a typical relationship of coastal lagoons relative to deeper ocean waters, and underscores the connection between lagoon dynamics, ocean water quality, and the health of offshore marine resources.

The team of scuba diving biologists from Merkel & Associates, including Steve Rink and Rachel Woodfield, saw something fundamentally out of place, something they had never seen before. They became the first to encounter *Caulerpa taxifolia* in the western hemisphere.

In consultation with the power plant, the biologists waited until after the July 4th weekend and then dutifully notified the city and affected resource agencies. Meanwhile, the team from Merkel & Associates lead by Rachel

Woodfield reached out to Meinesz via email. Had they detected and encountered the dreaded aquarium strain of *Caulerpa taxifolia*, the source of battle for their Mediterranean counterparts?

Despite the well-intentioned efforts of the scientific community and their Global Alert of 1998, Carlsbad's Agua Hedionda Lagoon became ground zero for the invasive marine seaweed within the United States.

A year and a half later, Alex Meinesz relayed a chilling story of prophetic insight to me. In early 2002, an international conference was held at a hotel across the street from San Diego Bay (which I cover in more detail later). The conference was a scientific call-to-arms so that the agencies, coastal managers, stakeholders and scientists aligned with SCCAT could benefit from the grave lessons of the Mediterranean experience. Meinesz joined other scientists and marine specialists from many of the affected Mediterranean countries, as well as Japan, New Zealand, and Australia. During an evening activity that included a sunset harbor cruise and dinner on San Diego Bay, I finally had my chance to approach him after a long and sobering day of conference presentations that outlined the reality of *Caulerpa*'s ecological devastation in the Mediterranean Sea. Surrounded by a cluster of professional and scientific colleagues at a window table during the harbor cruise, I introduced myself as representing the city of Carlsbad. Though he perhaps expected the mayor or city manager, Alex warmly welcomed me to sit next to him and told me his story that reflected his prophetic insight.

Meinesz told me that, after the Global Alert and the coalition letter signed by the global scientific community in 1998, significant progress had occurred regarding US policy in preparation for *Caulerpa taxifolia* sightings, and related care of aquarium contents. After a couple years of policy development at the national level, the awareness campaign was nearing its launch. As part of that effort, he told me about an American conference he attended in Washington, DC, during the early summer of 2000. As he related it to me, his tone was gracious and humorous. I could tell that, if anything, the conference really pleased him greatly, because awareness was truly being taken seriously in America, and many were working hard to make a positive impact.

At the end of the conference, he was asked to address the attendees and make some observations and summary remarks. He commended the participation of the conference attendees and the objectives of the pending action items. Given the very real possibility of recreating the Mediterranean disaster in the coastal waters of the United States, this threat was staring everyone in the face. He concluded by dropping a bomb: an infestation was already underway somewhere in our coastal wetlands. He challenged everyone to find the aquatic Trojan Horse before it was too late.

With a half-smile, half-sigh, Meinesz told me how the conference concluded and he traveled home to France the next day. After spending a day recovering from jet lag, he returned to his university office. That day, he told me, he was stunned as he reviewed numerous emails and came across one from the Merkel team via Rachel Woodfield, with the corresponding query and photos from Agua Hedionda Lagoon. He confirmed that *Caulerpa taxifolia* had been detected. Once again, his concerns and predictions had been intuitively correct.

Media Coverage: First Western Hemisphere Detection of *Caulerpa taxifolia*

On July 6, 2000, the first story of Agua Hedionda's *Caulerpa taxifolia* detection was published in the *North County Times*. Thus, the first known detection in the western hemisphere was announced to the world: "Killer Algae Threatens Lagoon—Carlsbad Estuary Is First in Hemisphere to Be Invaded by Organism That Damaged Mediterranean Sea."

Greig Peters, the environmental specialist with the San Diego office of the Regional Water Quality Control Board for the State of California, said, "This is the biggest threat that California coastal waters have ever faced. If you totaled all the damages that have been done by harmful pollution up until now, the potential destruction of this invasive alga dwarfs all of that. If it can't be controlled, it would destroy the entire coast."

The article pinpointed the cause squarely on the release of home-based aquarium contents that contained the invasive clone and ornamental plant. The impact to Mediterranean coastal areas was cited, as well as the corresponding economic impacts. While an overly optimistic timeframe of three months was estimated to eradicate *Caulerpa* through the use of underwater tarps and the application of chlorine, the severity of the situation was not over-exaggerated.

Bob Hoffman, senior biologist with the National Marine Fisheries Service in Long Beach and SCCAT member, was quoted as saying that the plant had caused catastrophic economic damage since it was discovered along Monaco's shore in 1984. By forming a thick, green carpet along the bottom of Agua Hedionda Lagoon, the plant could destroy the lagoon's native eelgrass, inhabited by many fish species. If it reached the ocean, the plant would further threaten vital offshore kelp beds. He concluded by saying, "If we were unsuccessful in controlling this and it spread to our major port areas in Long Beach and Los

Angeles, there could be a quarantine imposed on these facilities; it could have a dramatic economic impact."

The article announced the formation of a coalition between the affected resource agencies, stakeholders, and the power plant: the Southern California *Caulerpa* Action Team. Stakeholder John Davis, owner of Carlsbad Aquafarm, Inc., an aquaculture facility specializing in raising mussels located within lagoon waters, said, "It could destroy all the lagoons and could destroy our coast and our seafood. It's a killer algae, that's all there is to it. It's very, very bad stuff and we've got to stop it here."

The article concluded by describing the aggressive growth demonstrated by the aquarium strain of *Caulerpa taxifolia*. A single stem can grow more than nine feet, with up to 200 fronds. In ideal conditions, the diameter of a *Caulerpa* plant can grow up to 10 feet per year, with no known ability to slow or abate its growth over time.

Community response was a mixture of puzzlement and intrigue, while the response from resource agencies was one of strategic alarm. The power plant, under the leadership of David Lloyd, pledged diligent and financial support to assess the situation and identify next steps. At the city staff level, we felt like we stood in the pending path of a major hurricane—but without the benefit of a forecast. In many ways, as the city/SCCAT liaison, I was in the eye of the hurricane. Thus began an unwanted and unplanned relationship between various environmental agencies, the Carlsbad community, and the unknown dimensions of this destructive alien.

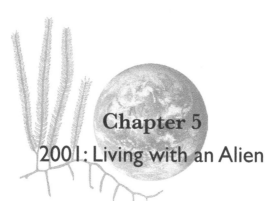

Chapter 5
2001: Living with an Alien

The second half of 2000 involved an ongoing dialogue between SCCAT and the Mediterranean scientists, including Meinesz. Confirmation, collaboration, and contemplation were our themes. Our mantra, "can not touch it," was repeatedly vocalized by agency staff, a fundamental lesson communicated from our Mediterranean counterparts. Indeed, it had taken them nearly 15 years to realize this simple truth. After all, what can a one-centimeter fragment do when it detaches from a frond? Well, in this case, it can find sediment, initiate growth, begin colonization—and advance an ecological disaster.

Development of the Eradication Technique

Early attempts to eradicate *Caulerpa* in the Mediterranean involved raking, hand removal, and vacuum-suction type efforts. However, these efforts only aided the spread of the algae, since they had not yet fully realized the meaning of "can not touch it" when it came to eradicating this plant. This led to the development of the underwater tenting/tarp technique, combined with applying chlorine to "treat" the area underneath the footprint of the tarp, secured to the lagoon bottom by sand bags. This technique does have precedent for treating aquatic invasive species like *Hydrilla* in California, but only in corresponding freshwater environments. There simply was no precedent, nor template, for marine invasive species located in coastal/saltwater ecosystems.

Furthermore, the development of an underwater tarp treatment and eradication approach in the Mediterranean was infeasible due to geographic extent. There is a logical limit to size and configuration allowances for the tarp methodology to function. The lack of ocean waves and the small scale area of Agua Hedionda Lagoon allowed for its development and implementation. An infestation on open-ocean reefs, or offshore kelp beds located outside the entrance to Agua Hedionda would have created a far different challenge, probably insurmountable. Thus, the importance and urgency of attempting rapid eradication efforts before tidal currents carried the algae into offshore waters. We had an opportunity to benefit from the scale and timing of our early detection.

The tarps were dark to inhibit sunlight from penetrating through the lagoon waters to prevent any growth underneath the coverage of the tarps. Some tarps were small in size for the smaller patches of *Caulerpa*, but the typical size was 18 x 50 feet in area. Larger areas were covered by using some increment of the 18 x 50 foot tarps. Typically a six-foot buffer was provided between the edge of the tarp and the corresponding edge of the *Caulerpa* patch. Tarps were anchored to the lagoon bottom by sandbags. Chlorine was pumped from the shoreline or boats.

However, we had a problem: funding. There were no funds set aside for an event like this. Why would there be? Unlike freshwater invasive species, or even an oil spill, there was no packaged agency response or protocols, no regime established to counteract the algae. Initially, the first funding came from the power plant. They had the business of generating power to maintain in addition to a profit motive, ample motivation to maintain the ocean-cooling water flows necessary for operation. Over time, grant funds were identified and pursued. However, the initial funding from the power plant is an overlooked element of our eventual success. As previously mentioned, the power plant retains ownership of the lagoon, unlike the other lagoons in San Diego County, which are under public agency ownership with corresponding challenges of staffing shortages, procedural bureaucracy, and chronic funding shortfalls.

Greig Peters inspired us by framing the situation in clear terms. He communicated the urgency for appropriate action that eliminated needless effort and set into motion our eradication response. He said this would be the collective challenge of our careers and that nothing less than saving the California coastline was at stake.

We Learn to Live with an Alien

Truly, 2001 was our first full year of living with an alien, a very challenging year of trying to understand the situation and provide effective action. At some point, every stakeholder involved felt the impact of the alien's presence. Scientists urged the closure of the lagoon. The business community feared economic impacts. Boaters and recreational users wanted to maintain water access. Surrounding property owners wanted to preserve their continually increasing values. Environmental supporters wanted to preserve the lagoon. A classic showdown of technical reality and emotional perception was quickly brewing.

During this time, media coverage accelerated, along with educational outreach from environmental groups. The March 2001 newsletter from the San Diego chapter of the Surfrider Foundation is a case in point. *The Surfrider Report* stated that the risk included "all coastal marine life." It overviewed *Caulerpa taxifolia*, the Mediterranean invasion, how it spreads, and what to do if you see it around the lagoon. It also outlined the threat posed to California's marine life, including kelp forests and fish species, marine mammals and sea birds. The article urged aquarium owners to not use *Caulerpa taxifolia* in their home aquariums, and to never release saltwater aquarium contents into a street, storm drain, creek, bay, lagoon, or the ocean.

Meanwhile, the eradication effort showed some initial promise. But it remained a very tenuous situation because another release of *Caulerpa* from an aquarium could restart the sequence of an established infestation. Other areas of the lagoon continued with eelgrass revegetation efforts; however, in some of those areas, new patches of *Caulerpa taxifolia* were detected. This process expanded the scope of the eradication efforts, which was viewed by many as being very daunting. I heard an analogy that it can be hard to get rid of weeds in your front yard, but we were going to do it underwater?

Besides outreach and educational awareness, a legislative tool was needed to outlaw the invasive seaweed and provide some basis for a prohibitive legal context, as well as enforcement at the ground level. *Caulerpa* was also available for sale via retail outlets and the internet, creating logistical issues.

An April 26, 2001, *North County Times* article noted the movement of a bill through the California Legislature in Sacramento that would impose a statewide ban on the sale, transfer, or possession of *Caulerpa taxifolia*. Assembly Bill (AB) 1334, written by Assemblyman Tom Harman of Huntington Beach, was an effective response to the need to provide a statewide ban on all *Caulerpa* species, despite looming enforcement challenges. Another obvious concern was that another lagoon or wetland along the California coast could become infested (or perhaps already was). The statewide approach was a prudent item in the legislative toolbox. A genus-wide ban on all *Caulerpa* species was considered more effective than a species-specific approach, because the latter would require accurate identification and distinction between various species from non-scientifically trained aquarists and the general public. There was too much at risk to isolate *Caulerpa taxifolia* for a statewide ban. Scientists across the board concurred that the importance of including the several "look-alike" species of the *Caulerpa* genus was necessary, and not overbearing nor redundant. (In fact, it can be difficult for trained phycologists and algae experts to consistently distinguish between the varieties of *Caulerpa* species.)

With AB 1334 bringing statewide focus of the *Caulerpa* situation, some entities questioned its need and warned of a precedent-setting process whereby other bans would follow suit. The Spring 2001 newsletter of *SeaScope*, for aquarium manufacturers, users, and hobbyists, ran an article on the ban in California and the recently introduced AB 1334. Written by Thomas Frakes, it reminded aquarists to never release non-native organisms into the environment. It covered proper disposal protocols for freshwater and marine organisms. The article concluded by stating, "Aquarists should be concerned that this issue could be the first of a series generic bans of organisms considered to be potentially invasive. Such bans could devastate the aquarium hobby. I understand the motive behind banning *Caulerpa taxifolia*, but I disagree with the extension of the ban to cover all *Caulerpa* species. The loss of *Caulerpa* would not cripple the pet trade, but it would be a dangerous step toward banning all exotic organisms. I encourage all concerned aquarists in California to contact their local representatives to let them know aquarists are concerned about the passage of Bill #1334."

Apparently, the perceived dangerous precedent of AB 1334 and devastation of the aquarium hobby trade was more feared by the pet industry than destroying native ecosystems and marine environments along the California coastline, which aquarium owners seek to replicate.

National Conference Presentation—Washington, DC

I had recently joined the board of directors for the California Shore and Beach Preservation Association (CSBPA), a statewide chapter of the American Shore and Beach Preservation Association (ASBPA). Since I had been giving several presentations to various groups, organizations, schools, and conferences, I was excited to speak at the ASBPA national conference in Washington, DC, during May 2001.

My presentations were fairly packaged at this point, covering the themes of coastal erosion, watershed planning, and invasive species under the title of "Coastal Issues of Common Concern." Every presentation covered the most updated status of our *Caulerpa taxifolia* battle; the national conference presentation was no different. The national interest in our efforts was very evident, and it was another professional highlight for me to bring this information to an American audience of coastal scientists, policy managers, agency staff, and elected officials at our nation's capital. I felt a growing sense of comfort and satisfaction with every opportunity to make a public presentation on the *Caulerpa* situation in the context of coastal zone management.

Lagoon Use Restricted for Eradication Efforts

The awareness of how easily *Caulerpa* can spread was becoming common knowledge. Correspondingly, it became obvious that the allowance for fishing and anchoring in the lagoon had to be restricted. East of the north-south Interstate 5 freeway, Agua Hedionda Lagoon is roughly divided into two zones for recreational use: an area from adjacent to the freeway to approximately the middle of the lagoon for power boats, jet skis, and water skiing; and passive vessel use like kayaking, windsurfing, and canoeing from the middle to southeast end of the lagoon. (Stand-up paddleboarding had not yet been introduced.) The active boat use area is also the location of the Hoover Street storm drain outfall area, where *Caulerpa* was first detected. Therefore, it was in this half of the lagoon that the Carlsbad Police Department enforced a newly enacted city ordinance that prohibited fishing and anchoring.

A July 5, 2001, memo from Police Sergeant Keith Blackburn (later a Carlsbad city council member) outlined the prohibition due to ongoing eradication efforts and the threat of spreading the seaweed from fishing or anchoring lines. The memo also contained a map of the subject lagoon area, posted in public areas around the lagoon and sent to all registered lagoon users. They, in turn, were required to secure a daily or annual use permit to enter the lagoon. The memo was attached to permit renewal applications and ended with an optimistic tone: "With your cooperation, and that of other lagoon users, we will eradicate this destructive algae as quickly as possible and reopen the lagoon to all activities."

Meanwhile, the rope-guided survey work to find pieces of *Caulerpa* in the murky lagoon waters was hard, challenging work. Divers would swim shoulder-to-shoulder with water visibility so low they could barely see each other. By holding hands they would squeeze their partner's hand when a piece of *Caulerpa* was sighted, and later mapped.

Full lagoon-wide surveys are very time intensive, requiring about 60 work days (when conditions and water visibility allow for dive teams to work). Full surveys are also expensive, approaching $300,000.

Just over a year had passed since the initial detection of *Caulerpa taxifolia*. It marked a milestone of sorts for SCCAT's accelerated level of awareness, action and progress in combating the invasive seaweed. It also marked a milestone of increased regulation and reduced allowance for recreational use. For the first time in the lagoon's nearly 50-year history, fishing and anchoring were specifically prohibited from a big chunk of lagoon area. While some could see it coming, others could not. This prohibition also foreshadowed a more significant and restrictive scenario that would involve a request to close down the lagoon completely. This request would be made near the end of year by SCCAT, but for now, the community was truly living with a very serious and unprecedented situation: an alien residing in our lagoon waters.

Invasive Species Draw Federal Attention

At the federal level, invasive species were receiving a high level of warranted attention and assessment. In a July 24, 2001, report to Congressional Requesters by the United States General Accounting Office (GAO-01-724), titled "Invasive Species—Obstacles Hinder Federal Rapid Response to Growing Threat," the clear connection between invasive species and serious threats to the economy and environment were outlined. Numerous examples and situations were cited. A revealing overview stated that federal rapid responses to invasive species that threaten agricultural crops or livestock are far more likely when compared to invasive species that affect forestry resources, rangelands, and aquatic areas. Within the realm of aquatic areas, it noted that freshwater environments had the benefit of some experience, which isolated marine environments as being especially vulnerable to impacts from invasive species.

The report outlined various challenges regarding invasive species and summarized a major obstacle: the lack of a national system to address invasive species. The solutions recommended were items that we were realizing and developing with our Carlsbad *Caulerpa* effort: integrated planning to encourage partnerships, coordinate funding, develop technical assistance resources, guidance on effective response measures, and initiation of "rapid response."

The concept of a national approach had just been the focus of a landmark conference in San Diego July 10–11, 2001, involving federal, state, and academic scientists, including some members of SCCAT. "*Caulerpa taxifolia*: Implementing a National Prevention Program" began in part with the Global Alert of 1998, the continued ongoing efforts of the Nonindigenous Aquatic Nuisance Prevention and Control Act of 1990, and the Federal Noxious Weed List, amended in 1999 to add *Caulerpa*. The workshop advanced the concept of a national system to address the specific situation of the *Caulerpa taxifolia* infestation. Workshop topics included: a Draft Action Plan to prevent the introduction and dispersal of the Mediterranean strain of *Caulerpa taxifolia* in US waters; regulatory authority; legislation; control and eradication technologies;

education; and an outline of Responsibilities and Roles for the Aquatic Nuisance Species Task Force—*Caulerpa taxifolia* (Mediterranean strain) Prevention Committee.

Meanwhile, ongoing eradication efforts continued at Agua Hedionda Lagoon, with summer recreational use proving to be a challenge for the consulting team. They had to contend with boaters and lagoon users while conducting underwater surveys to map out the precise locations of *Caulerpa*, installing underwater tarps, and the application of chlorine treatment. Diver safety was becoming an issue.

SCCAT meetings were held biweekly at the San Diego office of Merkel & Associates, and featured an update on the recent survey and eradication progress. The recent city ordinance prohibiting fishing and anchoring was appreciated, but the conflict of lagoon users with eradication activities was becoming more frequent. As the liaison between the Carlsbad community and SCCAT, it was becoming apparent to me that a more intimate dialogue with the city and lagoon stakeholders would soon be necessary. In fact, it could be argued that one element of the national approach that could benefit from our ongoing Carlsbad experience was to standardize the identification of local-based contacts to facilitate the technical interaction with "hosting" city representatives. This would weave together communication, trust, and effectiveness.

I sat in the SCCAT biweekly briefings and continued to be absolutely amazed by the display of intelligence and diligence by all involved. I sensed a pending intersection of technical objectives and emotional community dynamics looming ahead. As the summer wore on, I felt that the value I brought to the table would soon be put to the test, and that I would need the benefit of everything I had learned and witnessed up to that point when that moment arrived.

The One-Year Report

In September 2001, SCCAT issued its "One-Year Status Report: Eradication and Surveillance of *Caulerpa taxifolia* within Agua Hedionda Lagoon, California." It provided a status and update on the survey and eradication activities in response to the June 2000 detection.

With the benefit of a consensus to take eradication action amongst the federal, state, and regional resource agencies, combined with the immediate availability of resources, the Carlsbad situation truly represented the ideal "rapid-response" scenario. The resources available included emergency funds from the Regional Water Quality Control Board and Cabrillo Power, in addition to the field resources of the Merkel team. Initiation of eradication within a month after detection provided critical momentum for the progress and confidence of the SCCAT coalition. However, much was still at stake and unknown, as outlined in the One-Year Status Report.

The report outlined fundamental, significant progress in the eradication effort. However, our progress remained at risk if the eradication effort did not continue toward a comprehensive completion. There was a growing sense of urgency to approach the city council of Carlsbad, provide a technical update, and make a compelling case to close the lagoon to all recreational uses. In addition, funds for the eradication were rapidly dwindling.

The report noted that all previously detected *Caulerpa* patches were surveyed and accounted for by the end of summer 2001. A baseline of the situation and future eradication success monitoring was now in place. Continued surveillance efforts became more urgently important, and also more costly and labor-intensive, compared to the actual eradication program. All remaining patches of *Caulerpa* had to be identified and treated. A single undetected plant would negate any progress made through the prior eradication efforts.

The report also outlined the goal of a five-year effort, based on the results and status of the first year. Within the initial grid area of infestation, over 11,310 square feet of *Caulerpa* was identified, including 13 major patches (over 100 square feet each). By the end of summer 2001, the areal extent of *Caulerpa* was estimated at approximately 258 square feet within the initial grid area. In one year, we had eradicated almost 98 percent of the initial infestation!

However, we had no room for rest. Remember how a single centimeter of plant fragment is enough for *Caulerpa* to spread? Our focus turned to exhaustive identification of remaining patches. Since the sequence of repeated fragmentation leads to the expansion of its coverage, the report noted, "*Caulerpa* can move greater distances through dispersal of fragments by means that are not fully understood. In the Mediterranean Sea, *Caulerpa* is moved long distances by vessel anchors. At Agua Hedionda Lagoon, this mechanism, along with fishing, was identified as the primary controllable risk of spreading *Caulerpa*."

This set the stage to justify prohibition of anchoring and fishing by the city council of Carlsbad. It also highlighted the fact that the true areal extent of *Caulerpa* lagoon-wide, excluding the area at the base of the Hoover Street storm drain, was unknown. By the end of summer 2001, the lagoon-wide areal extent of *Caulerpa* outside the initial infestation grid was estimated at over 3,000 square feet.

We held an outreach meeting of the city's Senior Center, with the general public and various stakeholders invited. Two US Navy officers also attended. I noticed their serious demeanor throughout the meeting. Afterward, I went up to one of them, introduced myself and asked why they were in attendance. He looked me straight in the eye and told me in a dead-serious voice that if *Caulerpa* escaped our lagoon and entered the open ocean, it could travel to the port harbors at Los Angeles, Long Beach, and/or San Diego Bay, at which time every ship would have to be scraped of every mussel, barnacle, and piece of seaweed. It was quite a sobering response and reality knockout punch all at once.

With our focus on preventing any "backsliding" of progress to date, the One-Year Status Report concluded that continued surveillance would dominate efforts. With the larger areas of *Caulerpa* coverage greatly reduced, the emphasis was shifting to further identifying smaller patches over larger areas of the lagoon bottom. Necessary action included the acquisition of funds, since current funding sources were nearing depletion, and more coordination with the city regarding lagoon use and the consideration to terminate recreational activities. The report also established a benchmark to claim and conclude a full eradication: a minimum of two to three consecutive years of exhaustively surveying for *Caulerpa*, with no detection.

New Realm of Interaction and Dialogue, Engagement and Action

SCCAT took action on the contents and recommendations of the One-Year Status Report, preparing to enter a new realm of city interaction and dialogue. I could feel the moment approaching where the city liaison effort would undergo a defining flashpoint, and the community would need to "turn the corner" in its effort to succeed. Living with the alien was about to become uncomfortable and challenging, but there was no way around this looming reality.

The final three months of 2001 marked the most prolific period of community engagement, media coverage, and emotional expression. It began with an October 4 letter from the Regional Water Quality Control Board, on behalf of SCCAT, to city manager Ray Patchett. It noted the one-year milestone of eradication efforts, and requested the opportunity to make a presentation at the November 13 city council meeting to update the council and community. This was the flashpoint I felt. We were about to reach another level of engagement and action.

During the biweekly SCCAT meetings, the November city council item drew intense focus. By consensus, it was agreed that SCCAT would request two actions of the city council at the conclusion of the *Caulerpa* presentation:

(1) a request to the city to close the lagoon; and (2) a request for a $1 million contribution. I sat white-faced and stunned as this message was crafted for our council and community.

Obviously, the gravity of the situation made this two-part request seem like a no-brainer to most SCCAT members. It was not lost on me, either. However, I felt the dialogue would have to be more extended, carefully crafted, and delicately communicated.

Meanwhile, I worked on a side effort to pursue funding. I coordinated with Regional Water Quality Control Board staff to request $700,000 from the State of California's Water Pollution Cleanup and Abatement Account to fund the eradication effort. An opportunistic interpretation of a seldom-used section of the state's governing Water Quality Control Act, "Section 13442—Grants to public agencies," allows for access to funds to assist "in cleaning up the waste or abating its effects on the waters of the state." Our eradication and surveillance efforts were piling up costs at about $1 million per year; remaining funds fell short of $50,000.

Approval for the allocation of $700,000 was eventually granted on November 15, 2001. Working under a tight time frame and pending deadline, I drafted the city letter and secured the city manager's signature. It gave the city a chance to demonstrate cooperative goodwill to pursue potentially available funds.

On a humorous personal note, I learned that the effort to electronically "spell-check" documents still provided room for comical error. As I made copies of the city manager–signed letter and put it into the submittal process, I realized that my spelling of the word "public," to denote the city of Carlsbad acting as a "public entity" was missing one letter: the "l."

A Crucial City Council Hearing

Our preparations for the November 13, 2001, city council hearing brought the city leadership, staff, and community to the forefront of the battle against *Caulerpa*. While I urged SCCAT members to craft the council communication carefully, I simultaneously had to update city management on the pending requests that would be made of the city council. The issue of contributing $1 million offered a simple, unsatisfying answer: there was no excess city budget or fiscal reserves of that size (that would be applied to this effort). As for closing the lagoon? The city had no authority or jurisdictional power to do so.

Various city attorney memorandums were generated and management briefings conducted to assess the complex jurisdictional framework concerning the waters of Agua Hedionda Lagoon. The bottom line: there was no clear path for the city to claim authority for lagoon closure, a move that would result in vocal and emotional outcry from the lagoon community and citizens. Members of SCCAT were mostly scientists, coastal resource managers, and agency staff. They did not concern themselves with details such as being an elected official that had to maintain balance and credibility within the voting community. We'd reached the volatile intersection of community emotion and technical action.

On a workday leading up to the November council hearing, I was unexpectedly called into the quarterly management meeting by the city manager. Staff did not normally attend these management-only meetings. For some silly reason, I was more worried about not wearing a tie than the message I was prepared to give in support of my heroes on the SCCAT coalition. I was greeted with smiles and friendly joking as I made my way into the crowded room to sit near the city manager and city attorney. I knew that being calm would allow me to think fast once the questions started. I also knew, given the audience, that humor might be a tool for the occasion.

City Manager Ray Patchett started things off by saying that an upcoming council agenda item involved the SCCAT presentation, and that SCCAT would ask the council to close the lagoon and contribute $1 million. Muffled laughter and subtle snickering filled the air. He then turned to me. "Eric, why do we need to be concerned with *Caulerpa*? Can't the lagoon foundation go out on a Saturday morning and get rid of it?"

At this point in my city career, I enjoyed a great professional relationship with the city manager, city attorney, management, and most staff. I carried genuine respect for all, but my flashpoint had just arrived: I had to justify something at the outer edge of understanding for most of those in the room. I replied that *Caulerpa* is like a Frankenstein monster, and can reproduce through fragmentation. "If Frankenstein scraped against a light pole on the sidewalk, and a piece of skin fell on the sidewalk, that piece of skin would reproduce into a whole new being," I said.

The first response was explosive laughter. The second ran along the lines of, "Wow, we did not know we had cloning going on."

My comment and analogy of Frankenstein broke the ice. I felt comfortable . . . just in time for the real question: "Eric, we are going to be asked to close down the lagoon for all recreational uses. What you think of that? And before you answer, we want the city attorney to give us an overview of the agencies with jurisdiction regarding Agua Hedionda Lagoon."

City Attorney Ron Ball rendered a comprehensive overview of the lagoon's jurisdictional framework. He concluded that the city did not have "closure" authority. As I responded, I will never forget the deep silence that awaited my words. More than ever before, I had to maintain my credibility, and to a large degree preserve the credibility of SCCAT to our inner city team. At stake was a real chance to garner city support to eradicate *Caulerpa*, not just imagine it.

After duly noting the jurisdictional challenges at play, as diligently outlined by Ball, I outlined the physical dangers of subsurface scuba divers surveying for *Caulerpa*, carrying out the eradication program, while boaters, wakeboarders, jet skis, water skis, and other lagoon users shared the same waters. I lined up my concluding punchline. I slowly looked around the tables, scanning the eyes of the seated managers. "Nobody in this room wants the lagoon closed," I said. "And we are being asked to close it. I know there are legal and jurisdictional issues, but if we don't take part in closing the lagoon, then I hope nobody here holds their breath for it to get opened again. We will be told that we have no jurisdiction after all, and its closure will be done by other agencies. We will lose any negotiating ability for us to keep its reopening on the table."

Looking back, I can still feel the combination of shock and pride from various members of the city management team. I expected a confrontation between the city and SCCAT. What transpired, though, was something more positive: a two-way dialogue that put the lagoon first. While the city obviously was reluctant to see the lagoon closed in any manner, the failure to defeat *Caulerpa* promised a dark future filled with a devastated biological ecosystem and no recreational use. If the coral reefs of the Mediterranean Sea were no match for the threat of *Caulerpa*, how could our little lagoon hold up against such a formidable opponent? A deeper level of understanding and awareness was now emerging, just in time for the upcoming council item on November 13.

Nevertheless, the city position was based on legal underpinnings. Within a conservative context, it was prudent to allow the pending jurisdictional chess match to unfold. While the city held the ability to regulate recreational use of the lagoon's surface waters through the issuance of use permits, it did not have the legal power to prohibit it. In retrospect, this position allowed for a neutralization of the parties involved. Meanwhile, the SCCAT position remained firm: the lagoon needed to be closed to effectively complete the eradication program.

The media unleashed a flurry of coverage leading up to the hearing, announcing the potential lagoon closure and pending update by the SCCAT coalition. Below are some notable headlines leading up to, and after, the public hearing:

Lagoon Algae Eradication Effort is Out of Money | November 4, 2001
"*Caulerpa taxifolia* threatens to decimate marine life along coast."
—*North County Times*

Group Wants Lagoon Closed | November 6, 2001
"Experts seek Agua Hedionda closure to deal with algae problem."
—*North County Times*

Biologists Pursue Ban on Lagoon Activity in Algae Fight | November 8, 2001
—*San Diego Union-Tribune*

Businesses Wary of Lagoon Closure | November 8, 2001
"Hatchery owner says if boating banned, he can't use barge."
—*North County Times*

Residents Want Study on Lagoon Closure | November 9, 2001
"Homeowners: Closing of Agua Hedionda will affect property values."
— *North County Times*

Lagoon Algae on Carlsbad Agenda | November 12, 2001
— *North County Times*

Aquarium Owners Warned About Algae | November 30, 2011
"Fines for possession of *Caulerpa taxifolia* up to $10,000."
— *North County Times*

At the November 13 city council hearing, SCCAT presented with respect and technical accuracy. The orchestrated presentation and status update served both to inform and to reach out. Neither SCCAT nor the city council took a confrontational approach. While SCCAT was sensitive to the community, they pressed hard, given the urgency of the situation. Too much was at stake to be overly polite; however, a productive tone prevailed.

The need to control recreational uses on the lagoon clearly emerged. Aside from the safety aspect of scuba divers conducting surveillance and eradication efforts, there was the uncertain impact of water movements from boats, jet skis, and other watercraft, which could cause the *Caulerpa* to fragment and disperse further. SCCAT's preference to close the lagoon was very real. This initiated a new level of community concern and input. City council action focused on facilitating a meaningful dialogue between the community and SCCAT as part of an overall assessment of how to address the lagoon closure request. This resulted in two outreach meetings mandated by the council at the November 13 hearing, to be held on December 5 and December 11, 2001.

Community Input Floods Forth

The floodgates opened and community input gushed forth, covering the technical and emotional spectrums. We were in uncharted territory, a precedent-setting situation for any California coastal town. Or the Western Hemisphere. City council members were approached by various community leaders and concerned citizens. The media previewed the two workshops. On November 28, 2001, in a piece headlined "Algae Team Holds Public Workshops," the *North County Times* noted the purpose was to "explain the problems that the alga presents to the lagoon and the entire Southern California coastline." The article concluded with the summary that the SCCAT coalition asked the city to close the lagoon to recreational activity, but "the city council refused to do so, saying it did not have the authority."

It was becoming obvious that the two upcoming workshops at Kelly Elementary School, located within the north shore neighborhood of the lagoon, would become focal points on how best to move forward. Everyone thirsted for an interactive dialogue, based on non-emotional scientific integrity, without misrepresenting the financial aspects involved. Below is an overview of some communication that emerged from the community, reflecting an exhausting relationship between Carlsbad and *Caulerpa*:

- **Bristol Cove Property Owners Association**: The association produced and widely distributed green-colored handouts, the word HELP in large font letters at the top. Underneath, in slightly smaller font, it read: *Agua Hedionda Lagoon May Be Closed to Recreational Use Forever*. It was distributed prior to the November 13 city council meeting and represented one of the first community-based calls to readiness. It supported the eradication effort while also urging more information exchange and community dialogue so as to not close the lagoon without the benefit of such interactive efforts. Citing more than 50 years of lagoon boating, it mobilized a group of community stakeholders who would have an important and productive role in addressing the presence of *Caulerpa*.

- *The Watermark,* **newsletter of the Agua Hedionda Lagoon Foundation:** In a 2001 Special Edition (Volume 12, Issue 4), this newsletter provided non-emotional and factual information about the eradication efforts, its duration, and the upcoming November 13 city council meeting with a presentation by SCCAT. It also noted that the city would request two follow-up workshop events to engage and educate the community. It urged diligent participation and acknowledged the need for more funding. It listed me, Eric Muñoz, Senior Planner, as the point of contact between the city staff and the community, and my phone number. While calling on its members to monitor all upcoming events, it concluded by stating: "Hear and see what is being said, and let the City know your thoughts so they can take appropriate further action to safeguard the lagoon!"

- **Captain Bob Payne**: In a letter to the mayor and city council dated November 10, 2001, this 24-year Carlsbad resident and ship captain for 34 years, weighed in with his perspective: maintain the lagoon as a boating resource, but provide for the safety of scuba divers to continue and complete the eradication program. This perspective would become vocalized more as an alternative to lagoon closure. It touched on some side issues as well: the safety of the divers, the unfortunate loss of a longtime recreational resource, and the growing debate of whether or not vessels, and their propellers and wake, promoted the fragmentation or distribution of the *Caulerpa* located on the lagoon bottom.

- **Thomas Frey**: In a letter to the mayor and city council dated November 11, 2001, this Carlsbad citizen and longtime lagoon user felt that surface boats did not impact the *Caulerpa* distribution or promote its spreading in lagoon waters. He cited the continued boating and passive uses (kayaks, sailboats) and the cooperative attitude lagoon users had exhibited. He concluded by making the case for "shared use," and that long-held lagoon practices should guide continued efforts. Writing just two months after the Twin Tower terrorist airline attacks of September 11 in New York, he stated, "I appreciate this opportunity to convey my concerns regarding *Caulerpa taxifolia*. We can get through this similar to September 11th, if we don't react from a basis of fear, but rather from a well-organized and -funded program of eradication."

- **Sharon Glancy**: In a letter faxed directly to me via the planning department on December 5, 2001, Ms. Glancy represented a common viewpoint of nearby property owners: maintaining recreational use while completing the eradication effort. However, she was based in Long Beach, 80 miles away. She was also aware of the Huntington Harbour infestation. Her letter began: "I realize that the eradication of the killer algae is of great concern to not only those living in the immediate area, but also to the state of California, and probably the entire USA." She urged that future action take into consideration all parties and stakeholders involved, including those with property ownership interest in the immediate area. With regards to recreational use, she raised the distinction between power boating and passive vessels, foreshadowing another viewpoint that would emerge shortly. While clearly hoping for successful eradication and the continued ability to use Agua Hedionda Lagoon as a recreational resource, she concluded by stating that, if the lagoon must be closed, the same should be done at Huntington Harbour, in the spirit of safeguarding the California coastline. "Boats disturbing the water are boats disturbing the water, no matter where the water is located, and tidal water is tidal water," she wrote.

- **Nancy Bruce**: This Carlsbad citizen opened her December 13, 2001, letter to the editor of the *North County Times* with: "Do whatever it takes to save Agua Hedionda." She cited the rich biological marine resources and diversity of the lagoon and nearshore habitats. She also noted the situation in the Mediterranean Sea, and how *Caulerpa taxifolia* had defeated the efforts of those trying to restore life to that "once-vibrant sea." She voiced resignation at the option of closing the lagoon as "ecological wisdom to do everything we can to save our lagoon. I don't think we have time to do otherwise." She commended the Carlsbad City Council for making sound community decisions, then concluded, "Close it and find the money needed to continue the scientific effort. We don't want to go down in history as the people who lost Agua Hedionda."

The Kelly School Workshops

Held on December 5 and 11, the Kelly School workshops served as summits between all parties involved. Perhaps they should have occurred sooner; nevertheless, they provided a vital function for interactive communication in a face-to-face format. The scientists and agency staffers from SCCAT made their presentations and points, while the community countered with questions and declarations that reflected deep attachments to the lagoon. Property owners did not want eradication efforts to fail, nor did they want property values to slip, or recreational allowances to be lost in the long term. Wakeboarding enthusiasts strongly voiced their desire to carve up the most powerful and largest wakes their boats (restricted to 21 feet in length) could generate. Others expressed concern for anything that would even potentially promote the spread of *Caulerpa*. It grew contentious, emotional, vocal, and borderline rowdy during both workshops. I made sure to strategically position myself next to, or at least very near, the only gun in the room, which belonged to Carlsbad police officer Keith Blackburn!

My premonitions of the community's emotional and fervent questioning were playing out before my eyes. However, there was enough information exchange and mutual respect to sow the seed of a concept: to simultaneously secure diver safety and eradication program continuance, while creatively allowing for boating and recreational use. Some issues, however, would still prove challenging, like the debate of boat wake height affecting the spread of *Caulerpa*, whether to enact any recreational use closures, and related enforcement.

Reflections on Year One

As Christmas drew near, I reflected on what occurred in 2001, our first year of living with the alien. Grant money had been identified and secured to pursue the groundbreaking eradication program. The Agua Hedionda Lagoon Foundation emerged as a vital, credible community stakeholder with the role of managing grant funds, making diligent community payments to the eradication contractor, and serving as a neutral, apolitical resource. The issues of continued funding and recreational use came to a boiling point. The reality of *Caulerpa's* devastating potential was slowly becoming common knowledge, with the plight of the Mediterranean Sea serving as a sobering track record for marine resource jeopardy and failed human response. The idea of using scientific understanding as the foundation for future decisions, as well as honoring the concept of "shared use," would become vital reference points in our collective journey moving forward.

It was an exhausting year, but one full of milestones, accomplishments, and also shortcomings. All combined to provide a community experience befitting a globally unique situation. The main accomplishment was the continued activity of eradication efforts through the tarp-in-place technique. The fact that eradication action commenced shortly after initial detection was a significant difference from the darkly fabled Mediterranean reality.

Mark Thornhill, a political cartoonist for the *North County Times*, summarized the year's events on December 30 with his version of wit, humor, and cartoon art. Thanks mainly to the unprecedented and violent terrorist attacks on American soil on 9/11, the end of 2001 was a time for profound national reflection against an uncertain future. As part of "Thornhill's View 2001—North County Controversies Cartooned," he noted, "Looking back at 2001, North County trials and tribulations seem pale in comparison to the events of September 11." He reviewed twelve cartoons he produced during the year, one for each month. For November, his cartoon featured a sign in the lagoon waters that read: *Carlsbad Agua Hedionda Lagoon*. Underneath those words, the sign read *Beware Killer Algae*. A greenish algae leaf reached out from the water, its "hand" holding a pen that crossed out the word "Killer" and above it wrote "Terrorist." Now the sign read, *Beware Terrorist Algae*. The accompanying text added, "Some people say Carlsbad is snooty. Some say the city is too sophisticated. But any burg that stocks killer algae in its lagoons can't be all that uptight."

While perhaps a light-hearted way to reflect on a year of living with an alien, and the advent of national and global terrorism awareness, things could have turned out far worse. For me, the baseline objective of our *Caulerpa* reality had a global context: to avoid becoming like the Mediterranean Sea.

We had to seize the miracle and succeed. That would require the Carlsbad community, in partnership with SCCAT, to confront a challenge that had yet to be successfully addressed, navigated, and conquered anywhere else in the world.

Chapter 6
2002: *Caulerpa's* Community Challenge

Water can only get so hot before it starts boiling. Likewise, many dimensions of the *Caulerpa* challenge were reaching a boiling point as 2002 dawned. No one wanted to lose the lagoon: not agencies, nor power plant officials, scientists, consultants, funding programs, lagoon users, politicians, or property owners. Knowingly or not, we were all united in the desired outcome that only successful eradication could yield. This would be the year that revealed the full weight of *Caulerpa's* community challenge.

I like to describe 2002 as a year of "explosive passion": passion to save the lagoon, passion to seek scientific verification and comfort with the eradication program, passion to learn, fund, and maintain. On top of this energy was a global context that provided a distinct dimension of benefit and support. On one hand, the end of January 2002 would feature an international two-day conference on *Caulerpa taxifolia* in San Diego, attended by scientists and coastal managers from other countries, including a Mediterranean contingent led by our spiritual godfather of *Caulerpa* awareness, Alexandre Meinesz.

On the other hand, a personal and professional highlight loomed ahead. I was slated to be one of three American speakers at the first joint conference of New Zealand and Australian city planners, to be held in Wellington, New Zealand, in April. My topic was an updated version of "Coastal Issues of Common Concern" featuring Carlsbad's *Caulerpa* situation.

I sensed the boiling point in our local community: recreational opportunities, biological resources, and residential property values associated with the lagoon could not be lost to the invading seaweed. Stakeholders were sharpening their positions, SCCAT agency members were solemn and serious, and city officials and the Carlsbad community had emerged from the shadows of doubt, disbelief, and naive innocence. More than ever, I felt my place in the concentric eye of the swirling and breathing hurricane of *Caulerpa's* community challenge.

It Begins with an Update

On January 9, I provided an internal city memo to the city manager, city attorney, planning director, police chief, fire chief, and other city management staff:

January 2002 Update—Caulerpa Taxifolia

- **Public Outreach Meetings:** The December 5 and 11 public outreach meetings were summarized noting that over 80 attendees participated at each meeting including local and regional media coverage. A decision was made to form a citizen's group to initiate a dialogue with SCCAT.

- **Agua Hedionda Lagoon Recreation Users Group:** Seven community members comprised this citizen's group, and I was assigned the task of providing staff time and resources to their efforts. My memo outlined the members and areas of their representation: Passive/non-motorized users (Diane Richards), Power/motorized users (Michael Marsden), Commercial operator/Snug Harbor (Greg Rusing), Bristol Cove Boat and Ski Club (Keith Mahler), Bristol Cove Homeowners Association legal counsel (Wayne Brechtel), Carlsbad Boat Club (Mike Pfankuch), Citizen-At-Large (Gene Huber).

- **Lagoon Use Permits:** While the agencies wanted the lagoon shut down to eliminate in-water use, the city would continue issuing use permits, recognizing a new dialogue was commencing that may result in some form of recreational use restrictions. A fishing ban for the eastern portion of the lagoon, where passive uses were allowed, was put into place in late 2000 and remained in effect.

- **International *Caulerpa taxifolia* Conference:** I provided a preview of the first-ever conference to be held near San Diego Bay from January 31 to February 1, 2002, with international and Mediterranean scientists and coastal managers.

In the meantime, the city council and mayor's office heard from the community about the *Caulerpa* situation. Many letters came from Carlsbad High School, written by concerned students and representing an awareness of the situation's gravity. I was asked to draft a letter for signature by Mayor Bud Lewis (a former Carlsbad High teacher and coach), to Maria Tillitson, biology instructor at CHS. Dated January 11, 2002, the letter commended the students for their environmental awareness and outreach to city government. It noted that the spread of *Caulerpa* is no longer a threat but a reality, and that the city has "an opportunity to control *Caulerpa* in our lagoon, whereas there is little chance for control in the Mediterranean Sea." Various sectors of the city were sharing a commonality of impact and concern.

Just prior to the San Diego conference, a SCCAT meeting was held January 30, featuring another progress report issued by Lars Anderson of the US Department of Agriculture. The progress report noted that, since July 2000, nearly 20 colonies of *Caulerpa* were treated with liquid chlorine. Also, in early December 2001, core samples of the sediment within treated areas were collected and run through a strict protocol of monitoring after transport to marine labs at the University of California in Davis. Initial findings as summarized in the progress report (as of January 28, 2001), indicated that no *Caulerpa taxifolia* was reemerging from treated sediment samples. In fact, native eelgrass seedlings were beginning to appear, subject to further testing and monitoring.

This information was also made public. On January 14, the *North County Times* ran the headline "Lagoon Samples Reveal No Algae." The article reported that core samples from treated areas in the lagoon showed no sign of containing *Caulerpa taxifolia*. Lars Anderson was quoted as saying, "We will keep them for at least another month to be sure." The article also mentioned the upcoming international conference in San Diego.

This incredibly encouraging news provided an electric bolt of positive energy into the SCCAT effort. We had a hopeful, tangible signal of eradication success based on the immediate response action. With this update, there was a lot of anticipation, expectation, and intellectual energy within SCCAT going into the first day of the International *Caulerpa taxifolia* Conference.

Welcome to the Conference

When I walked into the conference lobby on the morning of January 31, I was overwhelmed by the sights and sounds. The visual impact came from the various poster boards and photos of *Caulerpa* in Mediterranean Sea locations, along with stacks of reports and outreach material that told a story of invasion that I felt I not only understood, but also had vested participation. The vibrant photos of bright-green *Caulerpa* overtaking foreign coral reefs on distant shores looked like tabloid photos of a mythical monster.

The aural impact came from animated pre-conference banter among scientists discussing technical aspects of algae morphology, *Caulerpa* locations, monitoring, and research efforts. What really struck me was the range of accents and languages extending far beyond the California tongue: Australia, New Zealand, the East Coast, Mexico, the Netherlands, Japan, Italy, France, Spain, Croatia, and others. This truly would be an "international" conference, and these people with their collective intelligence and *Caulerpa* experience wanted to help us kill the killer algae. I was overwhelmed with awe and appreciation.

The topics were full of information, a huge education for me. Scientists who had studied algae for decades were clearly astonished at *Caulerpa taxifolia*'s invasive characteristics. Its increased tolerances to light, salinity, and cold water temperatures were truly stunning, especially when combined with its rapid growth rate. Speakers addressed morphology and structure; growth patterns; various research and modeling efforts; summaries of invasions in California, the Mediterranean Sea, and new detections in Australia; management case studies; outreach efforts; and educational program efforts. It became clear to me that all the science and funding in the world would be helpless without an attempt to secure the understanding of the general public, elected officials, and policy makers, and of course the aquaria trade, institutional aquariums, and individual hobbyists.

A summary of some of the information presented over the two-day conference includes:

- Native *Caulerpa taxifolia* strains have small and weak stolons (roof systems) and fragile fronds when growing in low light and cold water conditions; the Carlsbad strain was noted as having a most aggressive growth structure and morphology, and actually flourished in colder water.

- All coastal ecosystems can be colonized by *Caulerpa taxifolia*: reef, rock, sand, mud, polluted, pristine, etc.

- Sea animals and plants don't like it or eat it, facilitating its rapid growth.

- Fish density is inversely proportional to the presence of *Caulerpa taxifolia*.

- A case study for Toulon Lagoon in France described the cold water winter environment there; the research team had no idea how it survived. Its persistent presence was described as "absolutely incredible."

- Manual removal allows recolonization, since the fragmentation of a one-centimeter piece can initiate growth in new areas.

- In Croatia, fishing nets were found to aid its spread and colonization. A threefold increase in areal extent was recorded in one year (1995–96).

- Native *Caulerpa* is found between Lord Howe Island south to Brisbane (Australia). However, around March 2000, fishery officials confirmed via diving that the non-native strain was introduced around Sydney. Detection triggered a national response process that included restrictions on fishing, boating, anchoring, and recreational use.

- In New South Wales, Australia, complete eradication is not considered possible, given widespread distribution; only a containment mode is a realistic strategy. Eradication was not initiated fast enough.

- In Guam, it was noted that native *Caulerpa* is readily eaten by herbaceous coral fish, and is actually a preferred food source for many fish in tropical waters.

- Open-ocean conditions of the California coast have higher and more frequent wave conditions than the Mediterranean Sea; thus the goal was to urgently pursue eradication within Agua Hedionda Lagoon and prevent any spreading via tidal currents to the adjacent open-ocean environment, where eradication would be infeasible.

- Much science and eradication precedence exists for invasive species in general, and freshwater aquatic species, but nearly none with marine invasive species.

- In Monaco, *Caulerpa* is the dominant marine plant. It took officials about eight years to officially determine its status as "introduced," and now it appears to be too late to realistically eradicate.

- In Tunisia, over 300 hectares were found with winter-water temperatures over 60 degrees Fahrenheit, so year-round growth and expansion is possible.

- Public outreach is necessary via various approaches, including media, school education, community events, dive clubs, signage, *Caulerpa* Day, etc.

- California does not have sustained tropical water temperatures to support native *Caulerpa taxifolia*, even with seasonal El Niño events.

- In Agua Hedionda Lagoon, credit was given to the power plant's private ownership of the lagoon (vs. public agency ownership) and the corresponding "fast start" to eradication efforts, along with contributing nearly $1 million in initial funding. To date, about $4 million has been spent in under two years. Many were amazed that recreational use of the lagoon continued while eradication efforts were simultaneously underway.

- After about 1992, eradication in the Mediterranean Sea was not possible; by the end of the year 2000, this has become a global issue: cannot stop it, can only watch it.

- The Conference proceedings are posted online at: http://escholarship.org/uc/item/16c6578n#page-31

During the conference, I had a chance to talk with Greig Peters, staff member with the Regional Water Quality Control Board who had been the leader of putting this situation into proper priority and perspective. It would be the last time I saw him; he passed away shortly after the conference. His role in saving our coastline cannot be overstated; he should be forever remembered as the driving force of our eventual success. He was the cardinal light of our inspiration.

As the designated representative from the city of Carlsbad, I fielded questions regarding our community's perspective. I emphasized several times that we were learning to not take the situation lightly, we valued the biodiversity and recreational opportunities provided by Agua Hedionda Lagoon, and that we were beginning a productive communication between our community and SCCAT.

A personal highlight was my meeting and one-on-one conversations with Alex Meinesz. This gregarious scientist held a deep love for the ocean—and a fair bit of sun on his face, which, for me, added to his credibility (as if he needed any beyond his research experience and authorship of *Killer Algae)*. Over drinks on a San Diego Harbor cruise during the first night, he related to me how Carlsbad was the "Trojan Horse" that I described in Chapter 4. I excitedly told him I was going to New Zealand in April 2002 to discuss coastal issues, including the *Caulerpa* situation at the first joint conference of New Zealand and Australian city planners. He signed my copy of *Killer Algae* with a positive note that foreshadowed our eradication success: "To Eric Muñoz, I hope that the Mediterranean bad experiences shows you how to better manage your local situation! I am sure that you will succeed!"

For me, it was a moment of pure inspiration, and also symbolized our partnership for ocean stewardship. My local role was now connected to a global context. It would empower me in many ways from that night forward. It is a large reason why I became compelled to write my story of Carlsbad's *Caulerpa* conquest.

Creating Lagoon Use Restrictions

A month after the San Diego conference, and after a few meetings of the Users Group, our growing objective became the creation of restrictions on recreational lagoon use: to avoid forced outright closure. The safety of the eradication team had to be secured immediately. This involved many sensitive discussions and negotiations. Zones were set up in the lagoon, which could be opened or closed on a rotating basis to allow for divers to continue with eradication and survey work. One of the issues involved the restriction on the height of boat and jet ski wake to 12 inches; this height was considered enforceable by city police staff. The idea was that larger wakes could generate downward energy in the water column, which might displace or move pieces of *Caulerpa*. This was not a light issue. But the alternative of a closed lagoon that permanently prohibited boating and recreational use motivated all parties to move toward consensus.

After public review of a draft plan, an "Interim Management Plan to Facilitate the Agua Hedionda Lagoon *Caulerpa taxifolia* Eradication Program" was developed and eventually approved by the city council on June 11, 2002. The three major elements involved a continuation of the ongoing fishing and anchoring ban for another year; a website with weekly updates and a daily phone call-in process, whereby users could find out which of the six user zones were open or closed based on eradication or survey efforts (usually scheduled around tides and water clarity conditions); and a wake height maximum of 12 inches. The plan was set up for monitoring and reporting to city council with annual review for assessment.

This was seen by the community as an incredibly positive step to not "lose the lagoon." While instances of challenging enforcement scenarios did emerge, for the most part it worked. The plan was touted in local and regional media coverage. In addition, the plan received awards from various coastal and environmental organizations.

Later, on July 30, 2002, with the Interim Plan in full effect, more good news emerged from SCCAT as reported in the *North County Times*: "Lagoon survey finds no new algae growth." While continued monitoring was cited as an ongoing necessary activity, there was hope that the eradication program was moving toward success.

International Conference: Wellington, New Zealand

Meanwhile, it was time to prepare for my April working holiday in New Zealand (Aotearoa, "the land of the long white cloud"), which would involve a presentation on "Coastal Issues of Common Concern" at the first joint conference of New Zealand and Australian planners. I was thrilled to be able to communicate to this large foreign audience our local coastal issues within a global context. It resonated deeply with conference participants. I spoke within a converted waterfront warehouse building, one of the oldest non-indigenous structures in New Zealand. Speaking in the capital city of New Zealand, a beautiful island nation which places a huge priority on environmental protection and invasive species awareness, was extremely rewarding. I especially enjoyed fielding questions from practicing city planners, university students, and a tenured university professor from Adelaide, on Australia's south coast. He liked the presentation on coastal issues including *Caulerpa* and said everything was very common—except they did not have *Caulerpa*. Shortly afterward, in August 2002, Adelaide detected *Caulerpa taxifolia* via an aquarium release into local wetlands through connecting storm drain systems. The thought of *Caulerpa taxifolia* also invading the coastal wetlands of New Zealand was depressing. The underlying gravity of *Caulerpa*'s spread was very sad and showed me that the monster can grow every day and nearly anywhere.

Another Funding Issue

Suddenly, funding the eradication program became an urgent issue. Due to the State of California's budget issues and diminishing sources of funding from various grant programs, no one was able to pay eradication contractor Merkel & Associates. A memo dated August 20, 2002, to the city manager and city attorney outlined this latest challenge, but shortly afterward, the State Water Resources Board secured the required funds. On August 24, the *North County Times* reported that "Alga Fight Funding Crisis May Be Averted." At stake was approximately $360,000 of billed work, with another $140,000 yet to be billed. This situation highlighted the issue of long-term funding sources for invasive species, especially "new" species that did not previously exist within an invaded area, or were not included within approved budgets of affected agencies or grant programs.

More Global Expansion of *Caulerpa taxifolia*

The funding issue occurred around the same time we received news about the Adelaide infestation. News Corp Australia reported that Operation Mutant was being launched in local wetlands against *Caulerpa taxifolia*—which threatened South Australia's $500 million fishing and aquaculture industries. The scope of Australia's *Caulerpa* presence now extended beyond the east coast of New South Wales to the south coast of South Australia. Mike Rann, the South Australian Premier, said, "If it continues to spread and escapes into the gulf waters, it could seriously damage the commercial and recreational fisheries along our coastline from the Gulf Saint Vincent to Spencer Gulf and Kangaroo Island."

Meanwhile, *Caulerpa taxifolia* reached the Mediterranean's southern shores. An article in the *Journal of Coastal Conservation* outlined its presence in Tunisian waters ("Extension of Two *Caulerpa* Species along the Tunisian Coast"). This article noted the extended ranges and detections of *Caulerpa taxifolia*, and also *Caulerpa racemosa*. While *C. taxifolia* was mainly found in the northwestern Mediterranean, recent reports noted the increased presence of *C. racemosa* throughout the Mediterranean. This triggered various monitoring efforts throughout the region.

New Detection at Agua Hedionda Lagoon

Back at Agua Hedionda Lagoon, our relishing of the no-new-detection media coverage of July 30 came to a screeching halt. On September 11, 2002, another patch was discovered near the north shore; it became known as the Boat Club Patch. While not large, it underscored the ever-present concern that "hidden" fragments of *Caulerpa* could go undetected. As it turned out, this would be the last sighting in the lagoon, but SCCAT team members and stakeholders still had years of surveillance before the assumption of success could be firmly established.

The year closed with more positive news and action. Consequently, the fishing ban within the passive use eastern end of the lagoon was being contemplated for removal. A Users Group meeting was held in November to provide an update on the Interim Plan and ongoing eradication efforts. During the same time, communications between SCCAT and the city attorney's office focused on the possibility of removing the fishing ban. On December 10, 2002, the city council approved the ban removal, subject to continued monitoring and possible recommendations to reinstate the ban if necessary.

The stage appeared to be set for the closing phases of the eradication program. *Caulerpa* was last sighted in September 2002; the Interim Plan allowed for the co-existence of eradication efforts and recreational use; fishing was now allowed in the eastern basin (but still prohibited elsewhere); and a work stoppage affecting the eradication program due to funding issues was averted.

SCCAT made it very clear that many years of follow-up monitoring would be necessary prior to any formal declaration of eradication. The community challenge was played out on various fronts, exposing our response and eradication efforts to regional, statewide, national, and global audiences. We had turned a significant corner—and, perhaps, had secured the upper hand.

Chapter 7
2003: Playing the Upper Hand

Less than three years had passed since we'd started our eradication efforts against *Caulerpa taxifolia* from a position of pure innocence and technical ignorance. Yet, we were able to accomplish the one goal that had eluded the Mediterranean countries and Australia by acting fast and launching our eradication response effort. The formation and actions of SCCAT were becoming a textbook definition of a high-performing team. Now, as 2003 dawned, most of us could sniff the possibility of victory in the air.

However, conservative prudence, combined with the all-mighty scientific method, would not allow for a premature notion of real success. A new level of commitment for follow-up monitoring vigorously searched for any new signs of *Caulerpa* in the lagoon. At first, we suspected that there were still colonies of *Caulerpa* hidden in the low-visibility waters of the lagoon, and we just were not finding them. Nobody wanted to risk or reverse the situation we had worked so hard to achieve. The initial size of the detected *Caulerpa* areas was approximately 11,000 square feet. Now it was down to an isolated area of four square feet near the north shore of Agua Hedionda Lagoon, per the last detection in September 2002.

On January 20, 2003, *The San Francisco Chronicle* published an article by Colin Woodard, author of *Ocean's End*, the book that included coverage of the Mediterranean invasion by *Caulerpa taxifolia*. Titled "California Joins Global Assault on Killer Seaweed," Woodard's article overviewed the ongoing battle in Carlsbad and provided a status update. It began by presenting a sobering story from Hvar, Croatia, an island in the Adriatic Sea where Starigrad Bay is located. It described the underwater presence of *Caulerpa taxifolia* as a thick meadow of luxuriant green foliage ". . . stretching as far as the eye can see." There, *Caulerpa* had covered rocks, sand, mud, and everything else in its path. The article noted that before 1995, "nobody in Croatia had ever seen this voracious tropical interloper, which is toxic to most marine animals and rapidly replaces other sea-bottom ecosystems. In the future, researchers feared, those diving off its Adriatic coast may see little else. Others fear California could be next."

Susan Williams, director of the Bodega Marine Laboratory near San Francisco, sounded the alarm of concern in northern California. "If, God forbid, *Caulerpa* comes to San Francisco Bay on somebody's boat anchor or (discarded home) aquarium water, there are areas that are probably warm enough to support it." Meanwhile, while reviewing the Mediterranean history, Woodard noted how some scientists and Monaco's Oceanographic Museum directors "dismissed the escaped seaweed as an amusing curiosity and expected the plants to die over the winter."

Instead, from an initial one-square meter patch, it spread to over 32,000 acres by 2003 via anchor lines, fishing lines, scuba gear, and other gear carried by boats traveling port-to-port. Alex Meinesz was quoted as saying, "For the Mediterranean Sea, it is too late. It can never be eradicated."

Woodard then aimed at the next target of outreach, education, and regulation: saltwater aquarium stores, where *Caulerpa* was sold as common aquarium seaweed. Sales of "live rock" were popular and contained pieces of stone housing marine organisms, including *Caulerpa* fragments. (Within the overall genus, *Caulerpa taxifolia* is one of 73 species.) Thus, while the 2001 legislation in California (Assembly Bill 1334) prohibited the possession or sale of nine *Caulerpa* species (three invasive, including *C. taxifolia*; and six look-alike species), the scientific community pushed for a ban on the entire *Caulerpa* genus.

Meanwhile, monitoring at Agua Hedionda Lagoon moved forward. Rachel Woodfield of eradication contractor Merkel & Associates told Woodard, "The battle is by no means won. We want to find no *Caulerpa* at all for several years before we can declare victory."

This was the strategic foundation for SCCAT and Carlsbad in our quest to achieve conquest over the alien invader within our coastal zone.

Meanwhile, reports on the invasive nature of the *Caulerpa* genus gained media attention in early 2003, even beyond the nine species banned by AB 1334. *Caulerpa brachypus* was the subject of a January 27 article from the Environment News Service entitled "Invasive Algae Smothering Florida Coral Reefs." The similarities to *Caulerpa taxifolia* included its non-native status, explosive underwater growth, and no natural predators. *Caulerpa brachypus* was first detected in 2002 an hour north of Miami, in Palm Beach County. Fueled by millions of gallons of sewage pumped offshore each day, the invasion of Florida's coral reefs displaced lobster and fish. Thousands of acres have been destroyed by "the green tide," with documented environmental and economic impacts. The article concluded that high-level policy decisions were urgently needed, along with corresponding budgetary provisions, and that leaders needed to take the threat seriously by citing the Mediterranean, where "government officials failed to act when *Caulerpa brachypus*'s cousin, *Caulerpa taxifolia*, was first found there."

Continuing the Hunt for Remaining *Caulerpa*

Aggressive ongoing efficacy efforts continued for any remaining *Caulerpa*. The story of *Caulerpa taxifolia* was shifting to a new angle: the brink of possible success. One example came from the Winter 2003 edition of *California Wild*, the magazine of the California Academy of Sciences. The article noted that some elements of the scientific and research community were longing for more opportunities to study this invasive seaweed, but those opportunities were nearly non-existent. As summarized by SCCAT member Bob Hoffman, "We'd love to be able to accommodate dozens of researchers, but this isn't a perfect world. Our focus was eradication."

The bigger focus? Not losing ground in the eradication effort. This meant using all resources and techniques available to confirm the lack of any remaining *Caulerpa* fragments in Agua Hedionda Lagoon. Keith Merkel of Merkel & Associates compared it to looking for a needle in a haystack, but "the needles were getting fewer and shorter, while the size of the haystack remained the same," he said.

The article also made salient points about the funding challenges, since costs for eradication averaged $1 million per year. It cited challenges in the Mediterranean and Australia, where the lack of rapid response resulted in situations that appeared to lack control or hope.

I continued to attend SCCAT meetings, and assisted with implementation of the Interim Plan to allow for recreational lagoon use while eradication and surveillance activities were ongoing. I also reviewed and processed financial payments to Merkel & Associates based on invoice criteria and accounting protocols associated with applicable funding sources.

Significant signals of progress defined 2003; namely, the modification of lagoon use restrictions. These were based on the pivotal issuance of the "Second-Year Status Report for the Eradication and Surveillance of *Caulerpa taxifolia* Within Agua Hedionda Lagoon." Prepared by Keith Merkel and Rachel Woodfield for SCCAT, and covering the time period of Fall 2001 through Summer 2002, the report was issued on February 1, 2003.

The overall report summary was quite positive: the quantity of *Caulerpa* was significantly lower than the Summer 2000 survey, which showed approximately 1,076 square meters (11,582 square feet). In Summer 2002, it reported an astonishing low 0.4 square meters (4.3 square feet)—a 99.96% reduction from the initial baseline survey data.

More precisely, the report outlined the quarterly amounts of detected *Caulerpa taxifolia* as follows:

- Fall 2001, 33.6 square meters (362 square feet);

- Winter 2001, 2.7 square meters (29 square feet);

- Spring 2002, 0.5 square meters (5.3 square feet); and

- Summer 2002, 0.4 square meters (4.3 square feet).

Clearly, the chlorine application within tarp covers was working as an in-place eradication technique. This led to a major shift in our focus from treatment to surveillance. Our new aim was to find remaining pieces of the seaweed through exhaustive survey and search efforts, so we could declare success with full confidence.

The report stated what was being verbally discussed during recent SCCAT meetings in terms of defining successful eradication: ". . . it is anticipated that at a minimum, *Caulerpa* must not be detected for two to three years before the lagoon would be declared free of *Caulerpa*." It concluded: ". . . it appears that success may be an attainable goal."

Another report element concerned a survey undertaken in June 2002 in the offshore waters north of the lagoon entrance, including Tamarack reef and associated kelp beds. The constant concern was that *Caulerpa* fragments would be carried out of the lagoon system by tidal currents and into the Pacific Ocean, where it would threaten local reefs. The June 2002 survey confirmed that the invasion was contained to the lagoon.

The update brought tremendous news. The validation it provided to SCCAT cannot be overstated. We now had a technical foundation to relax existing lagoon restrictions. It was a chance to demonstrate a major milestone of effective treatment, and also to put a spotlight on the need to aggressively continue surveillance efforts to seek out any remaining *Caulerpa* fragments. This kept funding sources in action, for they could not dry up at this important juncture. A primary message of the report was that continued surveillance would likely be more expensive and time intensive than actual treatment. The hope was that the September 11, 2002, detection would turn out to be the final sighting of *Caulerpa*. But the risk of missing remaining fragments in the low-visibility waters of Agua Hedionda Lagoon provided a continued source of haunting scenarios that inspired SCCAT members to temper any desire to prematurely assume full eradication.

Community and Civic Outreach Keeps Pace

Meanwhile, community communication and civic outreach opened up full-throttle. The City of Carlsbad website kept current with the situation, and the Interim Plan continued to be effectively implemented by allowing for eradication efforts as well as regulating recreational use allowances. I made sure the city libraries were stocked up with information cards on *Caulerpa*, the lagoon foundation updated members and kept stakeholders informed through their newsletter, and I gave numerous talks to local schools, civic groups, environmental associations, and city management. Existing restrictions continued: no fishing (except for the passive use area of the eastern lagoon basin); no anchoring lagoon-wide; and the limitation on boat wake to 12 inches in vertical height.

In March 2003, California Watersports and the recreational Users Group worked out a short-term goal with SCCAT: reopen the original infestation area to passive use only. While originally an active/boating use area, the fact that passive use discussions were taking place was hugely supported as a necessary step to reestablishing the active power boating use allowance. The recreational Users Group stated their support at a March 25 meeting, and the general public voiced support on April 17 at an outreach meeting. A few weeks later, on May 13, the Carlsbad City Council approved staff and SCCAT recommendations to amend the Interim Plan, including the reintroduction of passive recreational use to previously restricted areas. While restrictions on boat wake height, fishing, and anchoring were extended, cautious celebration ensued. Meanwhile, the stoic posture of SCCAT underscored the importance of continued surveillance, to help ensure no reversal or erosion of the progress achieved to date.

On May 14, the *North County Times* trumpeted, "Council Approves Lagoon Change. More of Agua Hedionda Will Be Open for Boaters." This front-page article covered council approval to allow for passive uses in the 30-acre lagoon area (Snug Harbor) where *Caulerpa*'s presence was measured at over 11,000 square feet in June 2000. SCCAT member Bob Hoffman described to the city council a phased reintroduction of uses to pre-*Caulerpa* conditions. The article summarized the work to date, emphasized the need for continued surveillance, and quoted the overt happiness and satisfaction of council members Mark Packard and Ann Kulchin over the current status and council's action.

"Snug Harbor Reopens; Fishing Banned," *The Coast News* reported on May 22. This front-page article, while covering the same points echoed in *The North County Times*, restated ongoing prohibitions on fishing and anchoring but noted that it was a big step for the community and SCCAT for the invasive seaweed that ". . . once threatened to consume the lagoon." Everyone was recognizing the effectiveness of the Interim Management Plan in conjunction with the eradication and surveillance activities. "If this stuff gets out of control, it'll be a disaster of monumental proportions," noted Carlsbad citizen Ann Russ.

Caulerpa and Carlsbad Go Prime Time on PBS and *NOVA*

Meanwhile, PBS aired a *NOVA* program on *Caulerpa* on April 1, titled "Deep Sea Invasion." It is available for purchase and viewing on the PBS website: www.pbs.org/wgbh/nova/algae.

The program opens with the observation and cultivation of the mutant genetic clone in laboratory tanks and then jumps to the invasion in Agua Hedionda Lagoon. The widely viewed show provided a forum to discuss and understand the issue, though many still questioned the adverse impacts of *Caulerpa taxifolia* and whether ocean ecosystems were truly at peril.

In this context, two camps formed: one that believed in the technical, environmental, and economic elements that warranted alarm and concern; and one that insisted that impacts were overstated and would not be of grave significance over time. A team of Mediterranean researchers led by Jean Jaubert, in association with various entities including The Cousteau Society, published "Re-evaluation of the Extent of *Caulerpa taxifolia* Development in the Northern Mediterranean Using Airborne Spectrographic Sensing" in the November 28, 2003, publication of the *Marine Ecology Progress Series*. It made the case that *Caulerpa* had taken root in niche ecosystems characterized by disturbed habitats, in particular sewer and stormwater outfalls with high nutrient content and minus the area's native seagrass, *Posidonia oceanica*. It showed the lack of endemic species impacts, pointing out the overstated areal extent of *Caulerpa* by other researchers. Furthermore, it noted a beneficial aspect of *Caulerpa* to filter and process the high nutrient content of those waters, a function the aquarium strain was actually intended to do, and why it appealed to aquaria hobbyists. Meanwhile, others noted the limited scope of that study, the lack of baseline conditions noting native *Posidonia* eelgrass areas for comparison, and other geographical areas adversely affected by invasive *C. taxifolia* that were not included in the study.

In other words, the two-way debate covered in the book *Killer Algae* had not ceased; it still carries on. Only time will reveal the extent of local, regional, or global scale impacts. Regardless, the quick response in Carlsbad eliminated that risk in our local lagoon. The Mediterranean and Australian waters (and not Agua Hedionda Lagoon) could become the test labs to prove if whether or not, over time, the impact of the *Caulerpa* invasion was overstated and did not warrant concern or action.

Active Recreational Uses Reintroduced to Agua Hedionda Lagoon

Meanwhile, we continued to play the upper hand. In mid-summer 2003, I was overjoyed to provide the most positive update yet. In a July 29, 2003, memo to the city manager and other management staff, based on recent SCCAT meetings and specifically a phone discussion with the SCCAT chair, I cited a pending recommendation that the lagoon be reopened to pre-*Caulerpa* conditions. I gushed with enthusiasm, thanked everyone for letting me be involved, and predicted, "It looks like Carlsbad will be able to put out the first global template on how to successfully combat this incredible seaweed." I doubt few people could have been more astonished than me. To be on the brink of success after what we'd faced just three summers before was, for me, almost beyond comprehension. Everything still hinged on continued monitoring, but if no further detections were made in the next two years or so, a formal declaration of eradication would be confirmation of our victory. State law identified the California Department of Fish and Game as sole authority able to make the declaration. And that declaration would only come based on a recommendation from SCCAT. A path to our goal was now in sight. No longer was it a far-fetched hope.

I remained involved in various strategy-development sessions that considered recent SCCAT input, the strong community desire to reestablish all recreational uses as soon as possible, ongoing recreational User Group interaction, and continued city attorney/city management communications.

Our various public outreach efforts, council updates, media coverage, and related SCCAT meetings culminated at a city council hearing on October 14, 2003. Based on staff and SCCAT recommendations, the Interim Management Plan was formally amended to reintroduce active water recreational uses. It still mandated the continuance of the Interim Plan, with rotating zones opened and closed to allow both recreational uses and surveillance monitoring by scuba diving teams. If any finds were detected, an immediate suspension of water use and reassessment of next steps would ensue. Nevertheless, this was a huge turnaround from the last three years of treatment and monitoring efforts.

Needless to say, I was thrilled to read the headlines and see the extensive coverage by San Diego–based network TV affiliates. The October 12, 2003, *North County Times* stated: "Lagoon Reopening Plan Goes Before City Council." On October 15, SignOnSanDiego.com proclaimed, "Powerboats Are Approved Again for Agua Hedionda Lagoon." In the latter article, I was quoted regarding the overall strategy of SCCAT in this phased sequence: "'The task force will continue to survey the lagoon quarterly, the council will revisit the issue annually, and the state Department of Fish and Game probably won't declare the area free of *Caulerpa* for two to three more years,' said senior planner Eric Muñoz, Carlsbad's liaison with the task force."

That was just a touch of the highly positive media and scientific publication coverage we received pertaining to our pending success—but also spotlighted the algae's looming danger elsewhere. In its October–December 2003 issue, *California Agriculture* published "Killer Algae Under Control, for Now." Susan Williams, director of the Bodega Bay Marine Lab of UC Davis, pointed out, "All lagoons in Southern California are at potential risk, as well as waters in Oregon, Washington, and Mexico." She added that San Francisco Bay is also at risk, since it is a destination for "live rock" (coral covered with living marine organisms used in the aquarium trade). Department of Fish and Game biologist Bill Paznokas, one of the primary SCCAT members, said, "People need to know they cannot release the contents of their home aquariums into lagoons and harbors."

Williams also authored a comprehensive document titled, "The Role of Science in Management of *Caulerpa taxifolia* in the United States." Her work further represented the necessary coordination of scientists, research, and reporting of data in conjunction with coastal resource management, funding, and policy implementation. The need for effective education and outreach was emphasized time and time again. This is where I came in: I vowed to keep outreach constant, the message alive, and prevent the *Caulerpa* story from fading into apathetic non-interest. I took every opportunity to communicate the lessons of *Caulerpa* in Carlsbad.

In the 2003 Sea Grant California Annual Report covering Sea Grant's response to *Caulerpa*, I noted their role in education and funding outreach. I provided the analogy of a house on fire. "The flames are gone, but the house is still smoldering. Likewise the eradication is not done." The Winter issue of

California Wild, the magazine of the California Academy of Sciences, included an excellent article, "Alien Alga, Keeping a Clone at Bay." It emphasized that quick action likely averted a potential disaster, but highlighted the need for eternal vigilance. The operative word was "eternal," for nothing less than constant awareness and monitoring would facilitate long-term success.

In the spirit and context of eternal vigilance, the *Caulerpa* Control Protocol was developed for the regulatory toolbox. It required a pre-project survey for projects that involved disturbance and/or in-water construction within Southern California wetlands, lagoons, or harbors. Certified personnel were required to make a finding regarding the health of any seaweed or eelgrass beds, and specifically determine the lack of *Caulerpa taxifolia* within a given project's in-water construction area. Years later, between 2011 and late 2013, as a private-sector planning consultant, I managed projects in a staff extension role for the Port of San Diego that had to comply with the protocol. It gave me personal satisfaction that such a long-term mechanism was in place, even if only for areas with proposed in-water projects. Surveillance of every square inch of the ocean, and every harbor or lagoon on every coastline, is obviously infeasible.

The year came to an eventful close. The Interim Management Plan received more awards and recognition from coastal and environmental groups, while the community reengaged with the lagoon and its pre-*Caulerpa* recreational activities. With a shift from eradication efforts to surveillance monitoring, the February 2003 Annual Report laid a critical foundation for reassessing lagoon use restrictions. While not completely done with the job of achieving the unprecedented eradication of the invasive marine seaweed, we set upon a linear path to find any remaining rogue fragments. In some respects, this was as daunting as the initial eradication efforts. Aggressive surveillance and monitoring would define the short-term focus of SCCAT under the hopeful eyes of the Carlsbad community.

Chapter 8
2004: The Search Is On!

Our positive momentum carried smoothly into 2004. On February 19, a joint news release was issued by some SCCAT-participating agencies: the Agricultural Research Service of the US Department of Agriculture; NOAA, via oversight by the National Marine Fisheries Service; and the California Department of Fish and Game. Co-written by SCCAT members Bob Hoffman (NOAA Fisheries), Bill Paznokas (CA Department of Fish and Game), and Lars Anderson (US Department of Agriculture), it was entitled "*Caulerpa taxifolia* Update— Group 'Cautiously Optimistic' of Eradication Efforts." Noting the last detection at Agua Hedionda in September 2002, it expressed cautious optimism that the infestation had been controlled. It praised the public/private partnership, the varied extent of involved stakeholders, citizen support, and quick action with regards to eradication activities. It anticipated a continued duration of approximately one year of continued surveillance, which could yield a determination of eradication. "Completion of this project would result in the first successful eradication of an invasive marine alga species. The approach of SCCAT is being viewed as an effective model for the eradication of invasive species," the release stated.

Newspaper coverage followed, with more stories like the front-page article in the February 25, 2004, *North County Times*: "Is Killer-Algae Effort a Victory?" SCCAT members stated that if future surveys conducted over the summer months revealed no further detections, then eradication would be declared. While excellent news, the message of eternal vigilance was also made clear, in this case by the USDA's Lars Anderson: "The caveat is that we still have to do some periodic monitoring. You can't just walk away and not look back."

A March 7 article in the Sci-Tech section of the *North County Times* followed: "Wiped Out? Multiagency Battle Against Invader Called a Model." It focused on the initial quick action that brought us to the brink of success. It credited the power plant and legal counsel David Lloyd for jumping into action with an initial $500,000 before agency funds came into play. Lloyd recalled learning of the Mediterranean's *Caulerpa* situation while reading a magazine in his dentist's office. Likewise, Rachel Woodfield recalled her astonishment when she first saw the initial patch of 11,000 square feet and estimated it had already been growing for a couple of years. Fortunately, beginning with the highly regarded Greig Peters of the Regional Water Quality Control Board, everyone recognized the situation could not be addressed via "business as usual." The article reported, "Where it grows, death follows. Fish won't eat it, and as it spreads, it smothers everything from rock reefs to sandy sea bottom, killing off native vegetation and killing or driving off native fish and all other aquatic life."

But *C. taxifolia* had never met a rapid response like ours. Due to that, and our innovative and effective eradication technique with the tarps and use of chlorine, the declaration of eradication could be made in the next year or so if pending surveys revealed no *Caulerpa*. In another article, Bob Hoffman indicated it would mark the first time *Caulerpa* or any other invasive marine algae has ever been eradicated. So throughout 2004 and into 2005, the search for new growth was on.

One new element that emerged: prioritizing other areas and wetlands in Southern California for monitoring. The Coastal Surveillance Program established a three-tiered priority system that ranked various coastal areas between Santa Barbara and San Diego. Rankings ranged from highest priority (#1) to medium (#2) to lowest (#3). Over time, however, available funds remained a challenge, since money had to be distributed between regional monitoring and surveillance at Agua Hedionda Lagoon (and also Huntington Harbour). There were new questions and challenges: How to deal with the tarps on the lagoon bottom? How to keep the buoys in proper alignment that divided recreational use zones on the lagoon's water surface? How to keep the dual activities of *Caulerpa* surveillance and recreational use operating in a safe and effective manner?

An interesting element of the surveillance effort involved the efficacy trials, essentially "tests" for scuba divers, deployed by the contractor team and Robert Mooney of Merkel & Associates. They assessed repetitive performance with regards to detecting *Caulerpa* fragments in the high-turbidity, low-visibility waters of Agua Hedionda Lagoon. Fake, plastic *Caulerpa* fronds were sprinkled in the water. The divers sought out the various sizes and quantities of the plastic *Caulerpa* to assess overall efficacy, the underlying confidence test being that, if real *Caulerpa* sprouted within the lagoon waters, it would be detected. The upcoming Summer 2004 survey would be instrumental in approaching the desired final outcome.

As noted earlier, data reporting was part of the scientific method being applied to policy implementation and decision-making. The May 19, 2004, publication of the Marine Ecology Progress Series was titled "Eradication of the Invasive Seaweed *Caulerpa taxifolia* by Chlorine Bleach," written by Susan Williams and Stephanie Schroeder. This represented a technical overview of the successful-to-date eradication technique at Agua Hedionda Lagoon, and served as an example of the need for science to use repeatable methodology so that eventually, a true eradication template could be developed that combined technical, legislative, policy, and community elements.

In July 2004, PBS's award-winning *Newshour* show broadcast a new segment: "US Battles Invasive Species." It featured interviews with Rachel Woodfield and Robert Mooney, who overviewed the eradication efforts at Agua Hedionda Lagoon. Carlsbad was again cited as one of the few places where people appeared to be winning the struggle against invasive species, after reviewing losing battles with invasive species nationwide. The takeaway message was the same SCCAT had been preaching all along: rapid initial response combined with the need for constant vigilance.

The year ended with two interesting items relating to *Caulerpa*. The first was a *Los Angeles Times* article about the fate of the tarps covering portions of the lagoon bottom at Agua Hedionda; and the second involved testimony provided by SCCAT Chair Bruce Posthumus (San Diego Regional Water Quality Control Board), myself as city liaison to SCCAT, and others urging for the entire *Caulerpa* genus to be added to the national list of noxious weeds—as opposed to *Caulerpa taxifolia* alone.

Addressing the Fate of the Tarps Along the Lagoon Bottom

The "tarp article," entitled "Killer Algae War Almost a Wrap, Except for the Plastic," presented the novel situation created by the eradication technique at Agua Hedionda Lagoon. While pumping chlorine underneath the footprint of the tarp, which killed off the invasive seaweed, a unique challenge emerged: what do to with the tarps still scattered along the lagoon bottom? Sediment collected on top of the tarps with accumulated marine growth, which supported a new ecosystem within the sediment consisting of eelgrass, sea sponges, and clams. Dismantling them presented new logistical and environmental challenges, while leaving them in place was seen as a bad precedent with regards to future situations that would involve habitat rehabilitation and restoration to pre-treatment conditions.

The total estimated areal extent of tarp coverage was approximately four acres (174,240 square feet). Credible viewpoints arose from both sides of the issue. Restoring the lagoon would eventually mean full removal of the tarps, while the case to leave them in place was based on a range of unknown elements associated with eradicating an aquatic invasive species. The California Coastal Commission would decide this issue. Combined with another half acre of tarps at Huntington Harbour, the estimated cost of removal was approximately $500,000, precious funding that could also be used for continued lagoon surveillance or baseline monitoring of the designated priority sites within Southern California.

SCCAT member Bob Hoffman summarized the situation. He stated that freshwater sites that have undergone system-wide treatments involved whole lakes being drained or treated with chemicals. Without an established tarp-in-place technique, and with saltwater, tides, and an open ocean connection via the lagoon mouth, there was no precedent on how to complete the current effort. "My opinion is we're probably going to do more harm yanking it out than leaving it in," Hoffman said. He also acknowledged the negative aspects of setting a precedent for "leaving stuff behind." While noting that SCCAT treaded new ground on this project, he also cited new challenges encountered along the way. "I don't think anyone's tried this technique before—isolate an invasive species by putting tarps over it, and then having to deal with the problem at a later date," he said.

However, tarps on the lagoon bottom would essentially prohibit dredging in the eastern lagoon area. The western outer area near the open ocean inlet undergoes maintenance dredging every two to three years, while the eastern portion requires dredging about every 15 to 20 years. The last lagoon-wide dredging effort took place in 1998. While the clock was ticking on this issue, we prioritized the ensured success of the eradication effort. Ultimately the tarps were eventually removed in 2006 and 2007 through an arduous effort involving scuba divers, rope, and boats.

More Concern About the Entire *Caulerpa* Genus

Given the media, community, and scientific focus on *Caulerpa taxifolia*, concern grew about the entire *Caulerpa* genus and its invasive tendencies.

At the end of 2004, I testified, along with SCCAT Chair Bruce Posthumus, SCCAT member Lars Anderson, and Ted Grosholz of UC Davis, in response to the Federal Register request via Docket No. 04-037-1 to solicit input regarding the List of Noxious Weeds. Our objective: to add the entire *Caulerpa* genus to the nationwide invasive species list. With oversight by the US Department of Agriculture Animal and Plant Health Inspection Service, our collective comments provided a sense of urgency. Bruce noted that it was one of the most useful steps taken to prevent future infestations, given "the difficulty in distinguishing between various species, subspecies, varieties, and forms of *Caulerpa* and because of the potential for species of *Caulerpa* other than *Caulerpa taxifolia* to be invasive, a less inclusive rule would be more difficult to implement and less likely to be effective," he said.

My input reflected my role in this multi-year situation. I cited my experience as working "in that interface between the technical and non-technical, and bridging the varying worlds of public expectations and scientific logic." In supporting the input provided by the SCCAT chair, I concluded by stating, "Taking action such as listing all the genus plants of *Caulerpa*, similar to making *Caulerpa taxifolia* a nationally outlawed aquarium plant and not just in California, seems to be a prudent and wise decision, whereas the decision of the alternative is too risky to play out into the future."

In a summary document regarding the petition and request for input, 43 respondents voted in favor (of which 26 were PhDs) and 16 against the listing petition (of which 2 were PhDs). Two registered no opinion. Seventy percent of respondents voted for it.

The summary went on to cite "notable quotes," beginning with Lars Anderson: "Having this plant anywhere in the US should be prohibited. There is too great a danger of people dumping this into lakes and oceans when they get rid of their fish and/or aquariums. This plant can and will cause us great harm if not controlled." Added Ted Grosholz: "Listing individual species, as California has done, has resulted in regulations that are entirely useless because of the difficulty implementing them due to problems with species identification." Other viewpoints claimed that *Caulerpa* only establishes itself in polluted or disturbed habitat, but the summary report noted the lack of confirming data in this regard.

Finally, I was mildly shocked to be included within the summary of notable quotes, listed as a senior planner with the City of Carlsbad: "I am personally and professionally alarmed at the severe destructive reality that invasive plants and animals are causing worldwide. Even more alarming is the human response, which has consistent patterns around the world, and usually center on 'over proving' a problem until the tragedy is so obvious, usually with economic impacts, that it only becomes evident after the window of opportunity for a realistic environmental solution has long passed."

The List of Noxious Weeds eventually was modified to include the entire *Caulerpa* genus.

Chapter 9
2005: Cautiously Sniffing Success

With the last new *Caulerpa* sighting in September 2002, and the results of Summer and Fall 2004 surveys forthcoming, everything appeared on-track for an eventual declaration of eradication. Meanwhile, after nearly 18 years with the city's planning department, I accepted a new position with Hofman Planning, a Carlsbad-based planning consulting firm.

Though hugely satisfied with my public sector experience and accomplishments, I was not going to remove myself from the *Caulerpa* situation, or from the community's eye with regards to Agua Hedionda Lagoon. In late Spring 2005, I made my transition to the private sector, bolstered in many significant ways by a month-long trip to Indonesia. My new focus was to become active with the Agua Hedionda Lagoon Foundation by getting on the board of directors, which happened in October 2005. By January 2006, I was president of the lagoon foundation, where I would serve for two terms totaling six years.

In 2005, the effectiveness of the Interim Management Plan continued to prove its worth, and its implementation facilitated continued progress with surveillance efforts while recreational use had continued allowances. Fishing, anchoring, and large wake limitations remained in place and were extended to June 2006. Along with that, agency funding was secured for outreach and educational efforts, since these efforts, along with "eternal vigilance," were considered a mandatory part of the overall response to the *Caulerpa* invasion. Prepared by Merkel & Associates staff, the January 2005 "Plan for Southern California *Caulerpa* Outreach and Education Program" outlined various activities and objectives that included database development, development of brochures, watch cards and outreach efforts, website development and outreach, and prioritized targeting of outreach audiences by organization and regional county locations. This served a vital role, but in retrospect, given the short life of available funds, outreach efforts represent an element of the invasive species response model that warrants more attention and financial backing. I saw a gap in what could be provided by city staff, the SCCAT agency staff, and contractor members. I became determined to give my energy to creative outreach and education efforts. This effort has taken many forms, including this book, to create awareness for invasive species and the protection of ocean resources and healthy coastlines.

My Parting Actions

In April 2005, one of my last actions as a staff senior planner was to extend the Interim Plan for another year, to June 2006. I also authored and oversaw the approval of a grant program generated by the payment of a per-acre fee for undeveloped agricultural lands being converted to development in the coastal zone, consistent with the city's General Plan and Local Coastal Program. Authoring this grant program required compliance with various coastal policy objectives and stakeholder outreach. In its final approved form, four criteria were developed for which the funds could be disbursed. One identified projects that would provide benefit for the city's three lagoon foundations (Buena Vista, Agua Hedionda, and Batiquitos). Years later, I would be on the receiving end of this grant program as the Agua Hedionda Lagoon Foundation secured funds related to master plan improvements for our center and trails development. It felt good to be involved with various connected aspects of the coastal portion of our community, but my main focus remained with the *Caulerpa* situation. I craved the day when eradication would be declared and I would represent the leadership and membership of our lagoon foundation.

Others were also visualizing that day. Many cautiously sensed victory and success. In *The North County Times* (April 11, 2005), SCCAT's Bruce Posthumus foreshadowed an eventual declaration of eradication. "That will be a good feeling when that day comes," he said. The article also introduced Josh Cantor, the new owner of California Watersports, the lagoon's waterfront commercial operation. Clearly, an eradicated lagoon with a clean bill of health would stabilize area property values, as well as create more profit potential related to business plan execution at the rehabilitated lagoon.

It was a busy summer season in 2005, as recreational uses fully returned to pre-*Caulerpa* conditions. The Interim Plan assured that surveillance activities could be carried out. Most felt that if the 2005 survey results were favorable (no detections), then success could be declared by summer of 2006. There definitely were some issues over securing adequate police enforcement for on-water compliance with the Interim Plan and the rotating recreational use allowances.

I made sure to maintain a presence within SCCAT via my new role as lagoon foundation president and was also very active, with continuing public speaking engagements including local and regional presentations, and planning and environmental conferences along the California coast.

In October 2005, a landmark effort was published with the "National Management Plan for the Genus *Caulerpa*" as submitted to the Aquatic Nuisance Species Task Force and prepared by the *Caulerpa* Working Group. This group included SCCAT agency members Anderson, Hoffman, and Posthumus, as well as Woodfield (Merkel & Associates), Alan Millar (Royal Botanical Gardens Sydney Australia), Paul Silva (University of California at Berkeley), Susan Ellis (California Department of Fish and Game), Susan Williams (University of California at Davis), Sandra Keppner (US Fish and Wildlife Service), David Gulko (Hawaii Department of Land and Natural Resources), and nearly three dozen others.

This document (available on the Aquatic Nuisance Species Task Force website: www.anstaskforce.gov) synthesizes all the technical and scientific lessons learned into a single policy document. The appendices provide an exhaustive and authoritative resource for literature review related to the Mediterranean/aquarium strain of *Caulerpa taxifolia*, and also a national prevention program for the Mediterranean strain. As an overall objective, the National Management Plan has the daunting task of combating detected fragments of *Caulerpa taxifolia* within US coastal wetlands and waters: if detected early enough, and if adequate action is taken by local authorities, and if funding and policy decisions are made in a prudent manner, and if . . .

Chapter 10
2006: Eradication!

After six challenging years, it finally happened.

On July 12, 2006, California Department of Fish and Game Executive Director Ryan Broddrick formally declared the two Southern California infestations of *Caulerpa taxifolia* at Huntington Harbour and Agua Hedionda Lagoon eradicated. Six years after initial detection at Agua Hedionda Lagoon, including three years of eradication activities and another three years of surveillance efforts, victory was clearly, confidently, and calmly declared.

The foundation to declare eradication was outlined in the "Final Report on Eradication of the Invasive Seaweed *Caulerpa taxifolia* from Agua Hedionda Lagoon and Huntington Harbour, California," prepared by Merkel & Associates, for the Steering Committee of the Southern California *Caulerpa* Action Team dated May 2006. The report (http://www.globalrestorationnetwork.org/uploads/files/CaseStudyAttachments/71_c.-taxifolia-eradication.pdf) overviewed the eradication and surveillance efforts, with total costs just over $4 million. (When you add in Huntington Harbour, the total exceeded $7 million.) The report summarized the now-familiar storyline of the mutant genetic clone seaweed cultivated for aquarium use; the initial patch around 1984 in front of the Oceanographic Museum of Monaco; the eventual spread to six Mediterranean coastal countries covering approximately 32,000 acres; the impacts to fisheries, tourism, and related boating restrictions; the detections in Australia; and the lack of any proven eradication technique available for replication in California. It reviewed the innovative eradication technique developed for Southern California, our quick response after learning from the Mediterranean experiences and scientists, and rigorous surveillance and efficacy testing. Eventually, it led to this declaration of eradication. Criteria for determining success included the verified containment and lethal treatment of *Caulerpa* at infested sites (with proven regrowth of native eelgrass), and the verified absence of *Caulerpa* at infested sites through exhaustive follow-up surveillance and efficacy trials.

Report recommendations centered on legislative efforts to ban the entire *Caulerpa* genus from sale, transport, and possession. Recognizing the enactment of Assembly Bill 1334 in September 2001 for nine potentially invasive species, including *Caulerpa taxifolia*, the report noted the need to extend these restrictions to the entire genus, due to much-cited difficulty in distinguishing between various species. The other major recommendation was to continue baseline surveillance in California for prioritized areas, in addition to implementation of *Caulerpa* protocol monitoring for construction and development projects involving marine waters.

Outlining the need for continued work, the report identified the necessity of removing the tarps to facilitate the regrowth of lagoon flora and fauna, as well as the critical role of ongoing outreach and education, given the possibility of a new infestation occurring due to the release of aquarium contents into coastal waters and/or storm drains.

Finally, the report noted the rapid formation and effectiveness of SCCAT, the procurement of funding, lessons learned from other global experiences, and the development of the in-place eradication techniques combining tarps and chlorine. This synergy resulted in a successful effort to eradicate a species of marine seaweed in a natural, non-controlled environment, where the unknown impacts of the invader reaching the open ocean were averted, to the amazement of many. After acknowledging the collective input and encouragement from the global scientific community including Australia, France, and Croatia, the eradication success was dedicated to the late Greig Peters of the San Diego Regional Water Quality Control Board, for his instrumental role in mobilizing and inspiring an effective, immediate response.

The media followed up with coverage that felt triumphant to me. Along with the community, they began to realize the magnitude of this rare achievement in the battle against invasive species worldwide. *The North County Times* on June 1, 2006: "The long battle to remove invasive algae from the Agua Hedionda Lagoon in Carlsbad is finally over." In the Op-Ed section a couple days prior, *The North County Times* awarded Roses and Raspberries to various local projects and situations. That included a "Sayonara *Caulerpa Taxifolia*" award:

A rose to the many people and agencies involved in successfully wiping out an invasive algae from Carlsbad's Agua Hedionda Lagoon. Later this summer, the scientists, government officials, and the public will celebrate a remarkable success story in the never-ending battle against noxious, imported weeds. Scientists figure the *Caulerpa taxifolia* algae first spotted in Carlsbad in 2000 was dumped out of someone's personal aquarium, and it threatened to spread throughout California. The effort to evict the algae from the lagoon has taken six years and about $4 million, but considering the devastation this pesky plant has wrought on the Mediterranean Sea and the Australian coastline, that's a bargain.

Capping local coverage was this June 2 front-page article in *The North County Times:* "Mission Accomplished, Algae Problem at Carlsbad Lagoon may Finally be Over." Summarizing the work and recommendation of SCCAT, Rachel Woodfield said, "We are confident that *Caulerpa taxifolia* has been eradicated."

An agency summary of the eradication announcement can be viewed online at http://www.waterboards.ca.gov/water_issues/programs/nps/docs/success/r9_eradication.pdf.

Years before, I literally wept at the thought of the lagoon being shut down for recreational use. I was not sad just because of the possible inability to boat, fish, or kayak. (Stand-up paddling was only beginning in 2006; but it would explode globally and become hugely popular in our lagoon.) I was more saddened that the ocean could be threatened by the "loss" of our lagoon, impacts to our native biodiversity, and the corresponding spread of *Caulerpa taxifolia*. It seemed like such a shame and waste, given the devastation that could result from a seemingly harmless release of aquarium contents.

The News Release We All Wanted

The news release we all wanted to write and issue came to pass on July 12, 2006: "*Caulerpa Taxifolia* Eradication—Officials Proclaim Victory Over 'Killer Algae' but Remain Vigilant to New Sightings." It read:

> Carlsbad, Calif.—Governmental agencies and community-based environmental organizations came together today to celebrate the successful eradication of the invasive seaweed, *Caulerpa taxifolia*, from the two locations where it was detected nearly six years ago. The algae, first detected in Agua Hedionda Lagoon (near San Diego) and Huntington Harbour (near Los Angeles) in 2000, is one of only a few known eradications of an invasive marine alga species.

Caulerpa taxifolia, also referred to as "killer algae" because of its ability to devastate and overwhelm underwater ecosystems, was popular in home aquariums and likely introduced accidentally into California's waters several years ago. Legislation in 2001 made it illegal to sell, possess, or transfer *Caulerpa taxifolia* and eight other similar-looking *Caulerpa* species in California. In other parts of the world, especially the Mediterranean Sea, *Caulerpa taxifolia* has rapidly, and permanently, displaced native marine plants and animals.

"The proliferation of *Caulerpa* in these waters would have irreversibly changed the ecosystem in California's near-shore coastal environment" said Tim Keeney, NOOA's Deputy Assistant Secretary of Commerce for Oceans and Atmosphere. "It was only through a rapid response and cooperative efforts of organizations at all levels that we were successful in preventing an ecological crisis."

The Southern California *Caulerpa* Action Team (SCCAT) immediately formed following discovery of the seaweed in 2000, to develop a plan to eradicate it from the two known infestation locations. The team is comprised of a number of agencies and organizations including the National Marine Fisheries Services (NOAA Fisheries Service), San Diego Regional Water Quality Control Board, Santa Ana Regional Water Quality Control Board, California Department of Fish and Game (DFG), the US Department of Agriculture, the Agua Hedionda Lagoon Foundation, and Merkel & Associates, the program's eradication contractor. The cooperative nature and scientific response utilized by SCCAT is viewed as an effective model for the eradication of invasive species.

"Invasive species can be like oil spills that reproduce, and can cause great environmental and economic harm," said DFG Director Ryan Broddrick. "Eradicating this harmful marine alga took quick action, collaboration, and hard work from dedicated professionals and volunteers. The Southern California *Caulerpa* Action Team helped make this a success and a model for future actions of this kind."

Officials continue to be concerned about possible outbreaks of the algae in other coastal areas and stress that it is vitally important to continue surveillance efforts throughout California and other susceptible coastal waters to ensure that other infestation sites do not exist. Sustained public education is essential to ensure there are no further introductions of this banned invasive species from home aquariums into our waterways.

Still, the members of SCCAT are relieved that this eradication effort was successful and hope they will not need to convene the team at a later date.

"Agua Hedionda Lagoon Foundation is pleased to host the celebration of the eradication of *Caulerpa taxifolia*," said Craig Elliott of the Agua Hedionda Lagoon Foundation. "The foundation will honor its mission of caring for the lagoon by continuing to support educational programs promoting awareness of the menace of invasive species and encouraging lagoon users to watch for evidence of new infestations of *Caulerpa*."

In addition to local TV coverage, other media coverage included:

Biologists Score Rare Victory Under the Sea | July 13, 2006
"For the environmental community, it's a rare happy ending. Global successes on knocking out exotic marine pests can be counted on one hand. 'We used to say it was impossible to do these things,' said James T. Carlton, professor of marine sciences at Williams College in Massachusetts. Carlton visited Huntington Harbour and Agua Hedionda Lagoon soon after the invasive plant was spotted. The successful algae eradication 'gives us hope,' he said." —Los Angeles Times

Biologists Defeat Algae from SoCal Waters | July 13, 2006
—KESQ and abc7.com

Killer Algae Invasion Crushed by Biologists | July 13, 2006
—NBCSandiego.com

Killer Seaweed Eradicated from Carlsbad's Agua Hedionda Lagoon; Quick Discovery and Subsequent Action Responsible for Successful Removal, Officials Say | July 13, 2006
—*Today's Local News*

Lagoon Gets Clean Bill of Health; Algae Declared "Eradicated" from Agua Hedionda—Announcement Ends Six-Year, Multimillion-Dollar Battle
July 13, 2006

"Calling it an 'unprecedented accomplishment,' a state official read from an official eradication proclamation Wednesday. 'You've protected the environment and eradicated an incredible pest,' state Fish and Game Director Ryan Broddrick told some 50 people at a ceremony at the Agua Hedionda Lagoon Foundation's Discovery Center."— *North County Times*

Obviously, I felt immense satisfaction and was hugely pleased to be the lagoon foundation president for this historic milestone. I was the lucky man who welcomed the community, city officials, SCCAT members, and media to the announcement celebration at our Discovery Center. In speaking to the gathering with Mayor Lewis and SCCAT representatives, it brought the whole experience full circle. I'd started from the public sector liaison role, and now embraced the community nonprofit role with continued outreach, celebration, and education regarding Carlsbad's *Caulerpa* conquest.

Finding Best Uses for the Surrounding Land and Securing Support from the Mayor

In my role as president of the lagoon foundation, I used my city relationships and community connections to make sure that the city, community, and foundation would realize the importance of this achievement. It didn't take long. During the summer of 2006, a land use issue emerged regarding the south shore of the lagoon and related open space provisions. It became an emotional issue. A citizens committee was formed by council appointment; each council member selected five people, as did the mayor. City councilwoman Norine Sigafoose appointed me to the committee. After our first meeting, I was elected committee chair by its 30 members.

Using a combination of my previous city staff experience and new role as lagoon foundation president, I presided over the recommendations that we developed and finalized. In November 2006, voters supported our recommendations after receiving city council support. When then-Mayor Claude "Bud" Lewis thanked me for my committee chair service, I told him that, over time, I wanted his support to keep the *Caulerpa* eradication in the community's annual calendar, rather than fading into a distant memory. I felt it would take at least 10 years for everyone to realize what we achieved. His support, and that of current and future city council members, was immediate and genuine.

With eradication secure, we focused on outreach, education, and enforcement of legislation and related laws intended to control *Caulerpa*. A new vector for the spread and dissemination of *Caulerpa* seaweed species emerged, including the availability of "live rock" to professional aquarists and hobbyists, via internet sales and e-commerce. A 2006 article in the *Frontiers of Ecology* journal, published by The Ecological Society of America, identified the reality and corresponding risk of invasive species being transported across state boundaries through e-commerce. The article documented the purchase of *Caulerpa* from 30 internet retailers and 60 internet auction sites representing 25 states, plus Great Britain. It went on to report that only 10.6% of the sellers provided the correct genus and species names with their shipments. This highlighted the risk of only regulating the *taxifolia* species within the overall *Caulerpa* genus through legislation and other attempts to control the sale, transportation, or possession of invasive seaweeds.

An August 13, 2006, article in the *North County Times* carried a similar theme: "Gone but not Forgotten: *Caulerpa* Laws Difficult to Enforce." Despite the declaration of eradication, the article communicated the very real fear that continued sales of the decorative aquarium plant for home use could make the region and other areas vulnerable to future invasions.

Citing the *Frontiers of Ecology* journal article, the *North County Times* reported that there was not enough widespread expertise between distributors and users to distinguish between legal or illegal products. Updated surveys showed that 8% of previously surveyed stores (in 2001) were still selling *Caulerpa* in 2006. The scope of outreach and target of related education now included retailers and aquarium shipment inspectors, and even suggested regulation of internet sales by eBay, which underscored the daunting task of preventing another invasion.

Despite the success of eradication, it would take effective and creative outreach, in addition to "eternal" vigilance, to maintain the hard-fought victory to eradicate *Caulerpa taxifolia*. The realms of creative outreach and public speaking, combined with repetitive *Caulerpa* conquest celebrations, would become my formula for serving the community.

Chapter 11
2007–2015: Celebration and Education

My role as lagoon foundation president, combined with my daily job as a planning consultant, created a very busy schedule. By far my biggest challenge was to effectively lead the nonprofit lagoon organization as we addressed various issues. We had to sustain and grow membership while seeking financial stability. We also worked to secure high-quality board members and provide direction to staff. With a newly opened Discovery Center looking westward over the lagoon waters, we had a high profile in the community and were striving to reach our potential with regards to members, financial stability, and overall credibility regarding lagoon stewardship and educational programs. For me, the obvious platform was to keep the *Caulerpa* victory on the front burner of our marketing and outreach efforts, highly visible in the eyes of the community, and a central focus of our various events and programs. That turned out to be a challenge of almost unexpected dimensions, and while later embraced, it initially felt like a vision that rested mostly on my shoulders.

As the summer of 2007 drew near, I wanted to host a community-based celebration to commemorate the first anniversary of the declaration of eradication. I approached Mayor Lewis to secure his support for the city's first Lagoon Day, slated for mid-July 2007. Once again, his support and that of the city council was complete and genuine. My idea was not to isolate our lagoon, but rather to combine the energy of the other two lagoon foundations for a Lagoon Day celebration. When I contacted the presidents of the Batiquitos (Fred Sandquist) and Buena Vista (Regg Antle and later Dave Billings) Lagoon Foundations, whom I had known for many years, I was pleased at their level of excitement and support. Each lagoon could promote their highlights, and ours would be the celebration of the *Caulerpa* eradication. I arranged for city council proclamations and related media coverage and earnestly worked toward putting a community spotlight on all the lagoons in Carlsbad.

I hoped this would blossom into an organically grown event every summer, but it was challenging to sustain based on my individual effort and enthusiasm alone. During some years, a walk/run event was associated with Lagoon Day. That occurred after the ability to have an on-the-water event evaporated because of the need to "close down" the lagoon to general public use in the July or mid-summer time frame. Such lack of access for water use, even for half a day to host an event, was understandably seen as harmful to viable business interests that provided commercial access to the lagoon and depended on the summer season. Thus it was requested that our water events only occur in October or later. So on one hand, the July eradication in 2006 managed to work against our ability to secure an annual summertime water event hosted by the lagoon foundation. On the other hand, a lagoon permanently closed due to an ongoing presence of *Caulerpa* would have not been able to support any recreational or commercial activities.

We always worked very hard to break even financially. The board of directors and staff rightfully questioned the prudence in pursuing events that did not provide measurable financial gain. Still, I was stubbornly frustrated that, given the global significance of our *Caulerpa* eradication, we could not easily secure adequate and consistent corporate sponsorship funding so our events could generate money.

That first Lagoon Day, in July 2007, received good media coverage, including local media outlets *Carlsbad Magazine* and the *North County Times*. "City's Lagoon Celebration Planned for Mid-Summer," the *North County Times* reported on May 16, 2007.

I still believe there is room to grow this concept within the city and I hope someday this seed can bear more fruit regarding a community-wide, annual mid-summer celebration for the lagoons of Carlsbad.

The Lagoon Day celebrations and related lagoon foundation events were unique. They kept the *Caulerpa* story alive within the fabric of the community. However, I resolved to pursue my own definition of effective and creative outreach by vowing to follow through with my dream and vision of writing the story of Carlsbad's *Caulerpa* challenge. Since the summer of 2000, I had fastidiously collected and maintained every city action, document, SCCAT action, and milestone, and nearly every print media item relating to *Caulerpa taxifolia*. Regardless of being able to establish a legacy of annual celebrations and Lagoon Days, or not, I would not let myself down with regards to telling the story from my point of view, and through words that would not require the review, consensus, or approval of others. The writing exercise would prove to be a source of happiness and healing therapy, with the end product—this book—providing a final source of closure and fulfillment.

Keeping an Eye on Florida's and Australia's *Caulerpa* Problems

Meanwhile, news of *Caulerpa* was reported from areas outside of California. In Florida, another species, *Caulerpa brachypus* (also dubbed "killer algae") was reemerging and taking over coral reefs in Martin County. On March 8, 2007, the Sun-Sentinel.com newspaper website ran this headline: "Killer Algae Returns to Martin County Reefs." Hurricanes during the Atlantic 2004 season had scoured the algae from the area, but over the past few years, a dramatic resurgence had occurred. The algae was blooming in 65 to 80 feet of water, and a 100-foot deep ledge off Jupiter Beach had 90% coverage by the cousin of *Caulerpa taxifolia*. Not good.

In Australia, the news sounded familiar, as these headlines pointed out: *New South Wales Bay Post*, May 11, 2007: "Noxious Weed Invades our Waterways"; The University of Queensland News Online, May 10, 2007: "Marine Weed Threatens Waterways"; ABC Online, May 14, 2007: "Weed Threatens Durras Lakes." An excerpt from the ABC Online article: "About 200 square metres of the weed is choking the life out of the lake. Friends of Durras' spokesman John Perkins is not sure if there is an answer. 'Unfortunately there has not been an effective way of combating this weed. A minor outbreak can break away and it can grow elsewhere. It can also last a week out of water,' Mr. Perkins said. He is looking to Government authorities for help."

I didn't want the same to ever occur again in Carlsbad. As part of my "creative outreach," I worked with new board member Jim Strickland and his employer, local company ViaSat, to secure a webcam mounted to our Discovery Center. My thought was that anyone in the world could view the lagoon that purged the invasive seaweed, and it would help lift our profile in various ways. We were also planning the next summer's event options, and I was always striving to have the *Caulerpa* story be part of our children's educational programs. I continued to make public speaking presentations at local schools and to environmental and civic groups throughout the region.

Comfort and *Caulerpa* on the Coast of Croatia

Then, in September 2007, my parents went on a vacation to Croatia. My dad always joked that I needed to visit that part of the world, even if the ocean there did not produce waves for surfing. The beauty of the Croatian coastline at Dubrovnik and Split is undeniable, and the Adriatic Sea can be stunning.

However, halfway through their trip, the unthinkable happened: my dad suffered a sudden brain aneurysm and died. Immediately, my older brother and wife mobilized to get there as soon as possible, while knowing Mom had good support from their tour group. Despite the horrific circumstances, Croatia cloaked me in a soothing comfort that I was not expecting. At 82, my dad lived a full life with no real health issues, and I enjoyed a tremendous, loving, and fun relationship with him. As I began to accept this tragic loss, I let the waters of the Adriatic Sea accelerate my healing by being near it, next to it, and within it.

After a few days, I realized something: Croatia suffered from *Caulerpa taxifolia* problems along its offshore islands. Split also was home to Croatian *Caulerpa* expert scientists, like Ante Zuljevic and Boris Antolic, who attended the international conference in San Diego in 2002. I visited a few dive shops along the historic Split waterfront and, working through the language challenge, asked about *Caulerpa*. Yes, they knew about *Caulerpa*, and that it was indeed a serious problem for some time now. Later I also learned that *Caulerpa racemosa*, another species, was a problem in Croatian waters. This was a sobering realization: that the stunning beauty of this sun-kissed coast could be harmed or altered by the silent invasion of *Caulerpa*.

Connecting with Hollywood

In 2008, I continued my outreach. I used the foundation's quarterly news-letters to spread the *Caulerpa* message and reach the community. I was also interviewed and asked about the lagoon at various community forums and events, including presentations to area schools, the Carlsbad Chamber of Commerce, Rotary Club, League of Women's Voters, Retired Military Officers Club at Camp Pendleton, Surfrider Foundation, and an interview with the *Carlsbad Business Journal.*

But the real milestone of 2008 came in the form of an innovative event, which for me defined "creative outreach." During the eradication effort, fishing restrictions were in place. Had *Caulerpa* not been eliminated, then fishing would have almost certainly been prohibited indefinitely in our lagoon. To celebrate a healthy lagoon, the concept of a fishing event developed. A significant twist emerged from one of our directors, David Danville, who somehow got hold of Hollywood promoter David Mirisch. Mr. Mirisch's own career was centered on getting movie, TV, and sporting personalities to be involved with charities. The list of charities he greatly assisted, by bringing celebrities to be part of their fund raising events, was very impressive. I had no idea we would become close friends through working on future lagoon events, and other efforts involving surfing and ocean-related organizations (a whole new world for him!)

On Saturday May 17, 2008, we held the first-ever lagoon foundation fishing event to celebrate our freedom from *Caulerpa taxifolia.* David Mirisch secured a dozen celebrities, all of whom were very active, gracious, and energetic with their participation. Many had been to Monaco and other Mediterranean coastlines, as well as Australia. Nonetheless, our *Caulerpa* story stunned them. The successful eradication impressed them enough to become engaged with our foundation's mission and the fishing event. They really felt like they were spending their time for a worthy cause and helping to promote the health of the oceans by celebrating our recent success.

One celebrity, Roland Kickinger, played fellow Austrian Arnold Schwarzenegger in the 2005 movie *See Arnold Run.* He was amazed by the *Caulerpa* story and afterward told me that fame and wealth have more meaning when they are able to lend their time and energy to good causes that make the world a better place. It showed me that all living people want to provide value in some way. It is hugely satisfying to become involved with something bigger than oneself.

The event featured about 10 boats in which competitors fished with a celebrity. There was also shore-based fishing, and fishing from private boats without celebrities. Prizes were given to the three largest fish caught among three species—halibut, croaker, and bass—in addition to children prize packages. The catch-and-release format event preceded a big party at the Discovery Center. All the celebrities spoke to the crowd, signed autographs, posed for pictures, and enjoyed a sunny day at our lagoon to celebrate the *Caulerpa* conquest.

Despite all this positive energy, some among the board of directors were initially divided on whether to develop and host the event. I lobbied hard and counted the votes just to get it approved and supported. Personally, I was in shock, and made it clear that we needed to have this event. Some voiced the opinion it was like having the Audubon Society host a bird shoot-out, even though we had a catch-and-release format, and we even had fish tacos at some of our board meetings! After scrutinizing the post-event financial summary, there was not enough energy and support to host a follow-up event. It was a huge lesson for me regarding perception versus reality, the ability for others to truly understand the significance of our *Caulerpa* eradication, and an enlightening lesson in organizational dynamics.

Nevertheless, the event was a huge amount of fun. I spent the day in a boat, buzzing around and checking on the fishing action while laughing and talking with fishing participants and celebrities. I communicated constantly with David Mirisch via walkie-talkies, ensuring all was running smoothly. It was very satisfying afterward to hand out $100, $300, and $500 checks to the winning fishermen, which included some local surfing friends. Everyone now knew about *Caulerpa* and its eradication, for sure! *The San Diego Reader* ran a cover with colored cartoon versions of some of the celebrities slated to attend, all fishing together out of a small boat. It was a level of outreach and marketing hard to pay for, let alone get for free.

One celebrity, Christopher Knight, became our spokesperson for several years. Many remember Chris well as Peter Brady on *The Brady Bunch*. To have such a friendly, genuine, and highly recognizable personality willingly be associated with our lagoon foundation was the end of the rainbow for me. I could not imagine a more successful effort at "creative outreach," for which I owed my new friend David Mirisch an endless amount of gratitude. Chris openly supported our lagoon, praised our *Caulerpa* eradication in related media coverage and interviews, and advocated awareness of the foundation for our role in lagoon stewardship.

Other celebrities that participated included Erin Moran of *Happy Days*, Christopher Aktins of *The Blue Lagoon*, Jerry Mathers of *Leave it to Beaver*, and nearly a dozen others. Related media coverage includes a video clip viewable on YouTube, "Agua Hedionda Lagoon Foundation Celebrity Fishing Tournament": https://www.youtube.com/watch?v=cVzbF2AotyQ.

The video contains comments provided by David Mirisch, Chris Knight, and myself. In addition, several other videos on YouTube feature fishing and other activities on Agua Hedionda Lagoon.

Finally, in the President's Message of the Summer 2008 edition of the foundation's newsletter, *The Watermark*, I wrote,

> On May 17, the AHLF held the first-known celebrity fishing event in Southern California. This unique event provided an unprecedented level of media coverage and exposure for the lagoon. With *Caulerpa taxifolia* cleared from our lagoon, the fishing event was our way of celebrating a healthy lagoon while also engaging a new group of stakeholders with AHLF: fishermen. When it comes to understanding the lagoon as a marine ecosystem, the local and regional fishermen who benefit from a healthy lagoon cannot be overlooked. The pure joy and energy of the fishermen (and fisherwomen and children) was very contagious and evident.
>
> Many expressed amazement at how an event like this had never been staged before and in fact we got input from far and wide (including New York!) expressing full support for our celebrity fishing day. The other aspect of this event was the celebrities who came to enjoy Carlsbad. Rounded up by David Mirisch of Mirisch Productions, we had over a dozen fun-loving celebrities who very much enjoyed their day on our lagoon. It was quite an eye-opener for most as they have driven by the lagoon but never got to experience or enjoy it. Another aspect of the day was to communicate the global precedent we have experienced via our elimination of *Caulerpa*. These celebrities are very intelligent and aware personalities: they understood very quickly the gravity of this situation and our corresponding success. At the end of the day, all involved felt that the positive momentum affecting our lagoon took a significant step upward and forward.

I was really pleased with the exposure the event provided, and how it raised the profile of our lagoon beyond our immediate region. Chris Knight agreed to be our celebrity spokesman for the lagoon foundation, and returned several times for our outreach and Lagoon Day events. Actualizing my dream of "creative outreach," this event was extremely satisfying for those of us who realized its potential from the start. The community provided positive feedback, and the city council was highly supportive. Nevertheless, citing the event's financial proceeds, the merits of involving celebrities, and other apparently related items, the voting majority of the foundation's board of directors made the decision to not host a second fishing event the following year. I remain hopeful that someday, the foundation can again host an event worthy of our fishing and boating stakeholders, and in honor of a lagoon that dodged the potential devastation of *Caulerpa* to our fishing resources.

A Trip to Australia

In November 2008, I visited Australia, fulfilling a longstanding desire to experience its coastal pleasures. I drove west from the south coast, starting with the Great Ocean Road in the state of Victoria, past Melbourne and Phillip Island, toward the east coast and up through Sydney to the Gold Coast, and finally on to Brisbane. It was a magnificent experience with kangaroos, koala bears, waves, weather, coastal towns, and remarkable wetlands. The south coast of New South Wales (NSW), bordering Victoria to the south and Sydney to the north, is studded with over a dozen estuaries and wetlands of high biological significance and biodiversity. From south to north, this coastline defines "stunning," with catchy estuary names of both English and aboriginal origin like Eden, Pambula, Merimbula, Wallagoot, Batesman Bay, Durras Lake, Burrill Lake, Uladulla, Narrawallee, Lake Conjola, Jervis Bay, Kiama, and Wollongong.

However, this beauty is being undermined with the *Caulerpa taxifolia* invasion that extends north, including Sydney Harbour itself. The government of NSW has a very informative and updated website that includes photos, maps, and information on *Caulerpa taxifolia* as part of its environmental programs: http://www.dpi.nsw.gov.au/content/fisheries/pests-diseases/marine-pests/nsw/caulerpa-taxifolia.

Around Sydney, the *Caulerpa* invasion was getting more attention. A marina expansion project had to consider if larger boats would stir up the *Caulerpa* beds growing underneath the surface waters on the harbor bottom. *Caulerpa taxifolia* was first detected in NSW at Port Hacking in April 2000, assumed to be from the release of marine aquarium contents. Subsequent detections were recorded in up to 14 coastal wetlands throughout the state of NSW. In September 2009, as part of a Fisheries Final Report Series, "Mapping the Habitats of NSW Estuaries" was published by Industry and Investment NSW. The presence and growth of *Caulerpa* is covered, as well as the related impacts to economy, infrastructure, and coastal resources.

Back in Sydney Harbour, a group of recreational divers participate in HarbourKeepers Marine Surveys, which monitor underwater fish biodiversity and maintain a weed monitoring survey with a focus on *Caulerpa taxifolia*. On June 29, 2011, *My Green Australia* published *"Caulerpa taxifolia*: the Silent Killer" and noted that despite extensive research and awareness, it continues to grow, affecting wetlands already stressed by urbanization, excess nutrients, and sewage. A lack of funding was cited as a chronic challenge, while the risk of losing native fish stock was (and still is) a very real threat. Dr. Gribben of the University of Technology in Sydney said in the article, "There have been no wholesale efforts to remove *Caulerpa* from very large areas. It just can't be done. There's just too much of it. Too much *Caulerpa* and it costs too much money." Meanwhile, bans and restrictions on fishing, anchoring, and boating are in various phases of consideration or implementation.

While on the south coast, I saw and photographed several signs that alerted the public, boaters, and fishermen about the invasive seaweed. I also noticed some areas had boating and fishing restrictions. It made me sad, and even angry, to see the grip *Caulerpa* held on these wetlands. One especially beautiful area was Fisherman's Paradise in the Lake Conjola estuary area. I hope it can live up to its name over time, since it is connected to the infested wetland waters of Lake Conjola. I wondered if there were concerned people who knew and cared, and who were mobilized into action. I was sure some people, agency staff, and community elements were aware and concerned, especially based on the many fishermen I spoke to. Still, it left me with a weird, lonely feeling along an otherwise magical coastline.

David Mirisch had arranged for me to meet two members of the Gold Coast City Council, north of New South Wales in the state of Queensland. As I concluded my tour of Australia's southern and eastern coastlines, I was honored to meet with Councillors Chris Robbins and Susie Douglas at their Gold Coast offices. These women represented Gold Coast Divisions 7 and 14, respectively. We had a very animated, wide-ranging discussion covering community topics including desalination, coastal erosion, and sand replenishment projects, artificial reefs, and the invasion of *Caulerpa taxifolia*. I told them of my experience with the Carlsbad community and council as a staff planner, liaison interactions with SCCAT, outreach efforts as lagoon foundation president, the waves and beaches that I was enjoying on their beloved Gold Coast, and my tour of the stunning south coast of NSW. I felt a strong sense of commonality with regards to assessing and maintaining "quality of life" and coastal resource protection at the local level, a goal of coastal communities worldwide.

One day, I want to return to reassess the *Caulerpa* situation in Australia. I would love to see a sister city relationship between Carlsbad and an Australian coastal city, or a sister lagoon foundation relationship, where an ongoing exchange of information, ideas, outreach, collaboration, culture, and students can emerge. I can never forget the value that we obtained locally from our interaction with Mediterranean and other global scientists. With worldwide awareness, we can be more effective at the local level. It makes sense to me that connecting communities with regards to stewardship, education, and outreach is fruitful. But it cannot be the dream of one person; it needs organizational and/or community-wide support to be embraced and implemented properly.

In the Spring 2009 edition of *The Watermark*, I provided my president's message to the lagoon foundation membership summarizing my Australian experience. In my message entitled, "Koalas, Kangaroos, and *Caulerpa*," I wrote:

> South of Sydney down to the border of NSW and Victoria, the coastline is studded with wetlands and waterways. The local Aboriginal name for this coast (Eurobodalla) means "many waters." In this coastal wonderland, about a dozen estuaries have detected *Caulerpa taxifolia* and of those, several have national park status and the reality of *Caulerpa* is in the very early stages. Talking with local people, there was awareness of *Caulerpa* and how it comes from aquariums and has a foothold in their estuaries and wetlands. Signs are prominently displayed urging boaters and fishermen to rinse off equipment to reduce the risk of *Caulerpa* spreading. With so many environmental challenges (abalone virus is currently damaging the coast/economy), *Caulerpa* seemed to be another one on the list. Seeing what it took to eradicate *Caulerpa* in Agua Hedionda Lagoon, and then gazing upon the expansive wetlands of NSW's south coast, it is hard to be full of optimism for the realistic eradication of *Caulerpa* in this beautiful area.

Within a year of returning from Australia, on August 1, 2009, I read a news report I never wanted to see. The *Sydney Daily Telegraph* proclaimed, "Noxious Weed a Threat to Fishing—A Noxious Weed that Could Threaten Fish Stocks has been Left Unchecked to Infest NSW Waters." A fisherman held a bright-green fragment of *Caulerpa taxifolia* attached to his anchor. Beneath the photo, the first line of the article said, "And now the State Government has admitted that the invasion by *Caulerpa taxifolia*—originally an aquarium weed—is so bad it will never be eradicated." Local fisherman Keith Sewell was quoted as saying, "There is no doubt in my mind that this weed will affect commercial and recreational fishing stocks because, wherever it's occurred, we've seen a depletion of fish." The rest of the article discussed funding issues, lack of effective action and rapid response, and the expanding geographic presence of *Caulerpa* and its impact. For me, it made our eradication success even more relevant and meaningful.

On May 26, 2009, the International Union for the Conservation of Nature (IUCN), operating out of Switzerland and representing 1,000 member entities and 160 countries, published "Marine Menace—Alien Invasive Species in the Marine Environment." It overviewed several invasive species situations in the marine environment, providing equal parts education and distress signals. Citing environmental and economic impacts due to ballast water movements via ships, aquarium releases, and other vectors of infestation and distribution, *Caulerpa taxifolia* was only one small story in a global problem without an easy or immediate end in sight. Once again, in searching for positive or successful stories in the global war against invasive species, our conquest provided a single example of success and hope with the message of rapid response, scientific oversight, funding, and community mobilization. At this point, the lagoon foundation's pursuit, and my personal mission of "creative outreach," made more sense than ever.

In 2009, we held another mid-July Lagoon Day event with the three Carlsbad lagoon foundations. While there still was no water-related event since the May 2008 fishing tournament, at least we kept the anniversary of the eradication alive. Again, there was strong city council support. During the proclamations at a council hearing in July 2009, I arranged for a commemorative acknowledgment of Craig Elliott of the lagoon foundation. He served an important role during the multi-year eradication and surveillance effort by "keeping the books" related to various grants and funding sources that partially financed the work of the eradication contractor. It required meticulous accounting, attention to detail, and adherence to various timing and reporting requirements. No one else wanted to do it . . . or really could. I was pleased to arrange for the retroactive tribute of his dedication and effective work, and the value he provided on behalf of the foundation.

The Lagoon Day Walk/Run Emerges

By July 2011, new energy developed within the Agua Hedionda Lagoon Foundation in the form of new board members and a new executive director, Lisa Rodman. There was more of a shared effort to celebrate the anniversary, including a new event: the Lagoon Day Walk/Run event. For three years in a row (2011–13), celebrity host Christopher Knight engaged with the community by hosting the Walk/Run event, which started on one of our shoreline trails near the lagoon mouth by the beach. Several community groups turned out, including the local high school film crew, the high school dance team, beauty contestants, military groups, celebrities secured by Mirisch, running clubs, and local corporations and sponsors. Local entity Tip Top Meats catered excellent food. The Walk/Run events ended at the Discovery Center, received press and media coverage, and satisfied my objective of "creative outreach," despite not being an event held directly on the saved lagoon waters.

Another event emerged on October 22, 2011, and was repeated on October 10, 2013, which did take place on the lagoon waters: the Lagoon Regatta and Poker Run. This involved various stops on the north and shore lagoon shores, and a barge in the middle, where participants picked up randomly selected cards to construct a poker hand. The best poker hands won prizes, including the top prize of a custom stand-up paddleboard shaped by local big wave rider, surfer, shaper, and stand-up paddler Scott Chandler. The participants got around the lagoon by kayaks or stand-up boards.

Since the event was held in October, we also held a Halloween costume contest. The sight of Regatta participants paddling around the lagoon in a variety of comical, creative, and/or eye-catching costumes was a most rewarding moment for me. Combined with slightly foggy conditions during the 2011 event, the sight of costumed paddlers making their way around the lagoon was amazing. Likewise, the support we got from California Watersports and owner Josh Cantor and his team was outstanding. The latent potential that we had been harvesting for years began to fully actualize. Chris Knight came back to host both Regattas. It seemed like the *Caulerpa* message, and the benefits of its elimination, were now tangible realities. The continued city and community support was also extremely satisfying.

I served as Walk/Run and Regatta event chairman and was very apprecia-tive of the overall support from the balance of the foundation board of direc-tors, executive director Rodman, the community at large, and Chris Knight for his energetic and genuine participation. Our community basically adopted him, thanks to his role at these events.

Therefore, during the July 2012 Lagoon Day recognition by the Carlsbad City Council, I arranged for a council proclamation to be presented to Chris for his support of our lagoon, foundation, and community. I was so pleased to see a signal of thanks and appreciation from our city council, and Chris diligently prepared an acceptance speech that addressed community spirit, the importance of our *Caulerpa* victory, and related protection of ocean resources. His concern for healthy wetlands and oceans, combined with the time he gave to our community, easily warranted our city's formal appreciation. Finally, I felt that our scope of exposure was not just limited to our city limits, or the boundaries of San Diego County.

I hoped that over time we could convert this exposure and energy into a new level of foundation effectiveness, fiscal stability, membership growth, and corporate support. Due to president term limits, I was technically off the board of directors in 2012 (although rejoined for another three-year term in 2013). Thus, I was touched and honored to receive the 2012 Volunteer of the Year award from the Agua Hedionda Lagoon Foundation.

Project Walk

Another event took place on April 6, 2013, that exceeded any of my previous expectations or ideas for "creative outreach." Located in Carlsbad, Project Walk provides a path of hope and recovery for spinal cord injury athletes. At this event, injured extreme athlete Kealoha Dime was incredibly inspiring with his positive spirit and active forms of rehabilitation. He was a role model in many ways. The purpose of the event? To have him paddle on the lagoon. This was the brainchild of local surfer David Kawika Watt assisted by Scott Chandler, and supported by Project Walk. Chandler crafted a stand-up paddleboard and modified it with indented deck channels and outrigger-style pontoons that al-lowed us to strap Dime's wheelchair to the deck of the board after using a wheeled ramp system to cross the sand. Once strapped in, Kealoha amazed us with his smooth, confident paddle strokes. A throng of local paddlers and surfers soon joined him. Together, we paddled along the north shore on kayaks, surfboards, and stand-up paddleboards. It ended with a big celebration at Cali-fornia Water Sports that included participation by Mayor Matt Hall.

For those who got to paddle next to Dime on the water, including me, it was a transformative and spiritual experience. We crossed a huge boundary and barrier with regards to lagoon access and formed a new definition of spinal cord recovery. Now that we had healed the lagoon, the lagoon in turn was providing an unprecedented level of healing to humans. It was another uncharted milestone for our local lagoon to showcase to the world.

In addition to media coverage, I also wrote short articles for the online version of the *San Diego Reader* to expand lagoon exposure and to continue our outreach and education related to our *Caulerpa* eradication. These included: "*Caulerpa* Conquest to be Celebrated in Carlsbad," July 19, 2012; "Agua Hedionda Lagoon Hosts Paddle for Injured Athlete—Standup Board Modified for Wheelchair," April 10, 2013; "Poker Game on Agua Hedionda Lagoon—In Celebration of Conquered Seaweed," October 21, 2013. Links for these articles are provided below:

- www.sandiegoreader.com/news/2012/jul/19/stringers-caulerpa-conquest-be-celebrated-/
- www.sandiegoreader.com/news/2013/apr/10/stringers-agua-hedionda-lagoon-hosts-/
- www.sandiegoreader.com/news/2013/oct/21/stringers-poker-game-agua-hedionda/

Once again, the scrutiny of financial gain and foundation proceeds, the assessment of time and logistic efforts relative to benefit, and related analysis of various post-event metrics were a sobering counterbalance to the contagious excitement of the events themselves. There is never a shortage of life lessons when it comes to organizational pursuits, fundraising, community dynamics, leadership, or lagoon stewardship.

Continually Seeking Funding, Reminding People of What Might Have Been

By 2014, stand-up paddling exploded in popularity throughout global waters, and certainly within Agua Hedionda Lagoon. We continued to seek ways to fundraise and make our organization fiscally strong. I always thought that if we could get one dollar for every paddle that touched our lagoon, we would be the most well-funded organization anywhere. However, newer generations of lagoon users have mostly not heard, nor realized the seriousness, of the *Caulerpa* success story that now allows for their on-water lagoon enjoyment. While on city staff, I developed a mindset and phrase for dealing with community issues, and the general public, that "tragedy is the only real agent of change." Perhaps the tragedy here was not tragic enough. Had the lagoon been actually closed down, then the efforts of the lagoon foundation and the city to keep it open would have developed a different tone and context.

With our successful outcome, the challenge now seems to be mobilizing citizen and corporate interests to support the Agua Hedionda Lagoon Foundation, as opposed to adopting hypnotic apathy. In 2014, our walk/run event was moved from a July Lagoon Day time frame to World Water Day in March. The annual memorialization of the eradication anniversary in July had missed a beat.

During 2014 I was looking for ways to continue my previous commitment for "creative outreach" and to stay involved and engaged with spreading the *Caulerpa* message. No one was asking for speaking presentations anymore, and while I am sure *Caulerpa* got a mention in our foundation's outreach activities and education programs for school children, my own sense was that I had to conjure up something to satisfy my own definition of performance regarding creative outreach. That is why I had been slowly drafting my story for this book over the years, following a carefully crafted outline of the chronological sequence of related events and milestones.

Suddenly, an unexpected collaboration with a close surfing friend soon provided that level of satisfaction for which I was deeply thirsting.

The TED Video

Eli Enigenburg is a Carlsbad-based freelance computer graphics animator. We enjoyed many local and distant waves and laughs. One day, he showed me a TED animated video he produced on cicadas, an odd underground insect that invades Midwest and southern farm crops and forests in 17-year cycles, destroying crops and puncturing quiet days and nights with their shrill, sharp screams. An TED Educator wrote a short script, a voice professionally narrated, and Eli provided the graphic animation. I was stunned at my friend's creative talent and the smooth visuals he provided to augment the video's narrated script. When I mentioned that this format would be perfect to tell the *Caulerpa* story, he simply smiled. "That's why I showed it to you," he said.

We embarked on our collaboration. We drafted an outline telling the story and made our submission online to TED. Within two weeks, I received a positive email response. A week later, I found myself on a phone interview with a director and his team from TED in New York. I was so thrilled that someone wanted to hear the *Caulerpa* story from its Mediterranean beginning, to our local efforts and related global implications. They were amazed. Eli and I were given the green light to work together; over time, we developed our script. I provided narration in Eli's sound studio, and we shared many energetic discussions about the creation of animated visual graphics to correspond with our script. Eli's work easily surpassed my expectations. I was so excited to be involved with this effort.

On June 24, 2014, our animated video was released worldwide via TED and YouTube online channels. Subtitles became available in about 12 languages, enabling us to reach an online global audience that could have never happened in a different, conventional, or non-online format. Teachers show or customize it for classroom instruction, based in part on discussion questions I developed to accompany the video. You can view it by going to www.youtube.com/watch?v=Vd4rgN6MYtg, or at www.ed.ted.com/lessons/attack-of-the-killer-algae-eric-noel-Muñoz.

The video, in an entertaining format, provides a three-minute overview of the *Caulerpa* eradication in Carlsbad, with a review of the Mediterranean situation and its presence in Australian waters. We covered the lessons and issues of invasive species, aquarium releases, and genetic cloning. It was my intention that this video would become a standardized element of the Agua Hedionda Lagoon Foundation's educational program for children. It is also linked at our lagoon foundation website http://aguahedionda.org.

Being able to share this video as a TED Educator has been hugely satisfying because I can talk about *Caulerpa* with someone, anywhere, and can ask if they have a phone with internet access. I can show them the video, right then and there. It is very modern, and effective. I remain super grateful to Eli for this opportunity, which left me more inspired than ever to finalize my book effort.

I thought about how to conclude my story. Building on the excitement of the TED video, I thought about the current status of *Caulerpa* in Australia, Croatia, and the balance of the Mediterranean. *Is it still a huge problem? Is it still there? How about the scientists I knew years ago at the international conference in San Diego?* As I planned a vacation for 2015, already intrigued with surfing some waves in the Mediterranean Sea (while also bringing my inflatable stand-up board to paddle the canals of Venice), I stared intensely at a map of Italy. Then it hit me like a rock: I needed to make my own pilgrimage to ground zero, Monaco, to the Oceanographic Museum and aquarium, and to the adjacent coast of the French Riviera. I wanted to see *Caulerpa taxifolia* with my own eyes in Mediterranean waters.

Return to the Source

Inflamed with new purpose and energy, I planned a longer trip to Italy so that I could spend some time in Monaco. I was inspired. I reconnected with local *Caulerpa* warriors Rachel Woodfield and Robert Mooney, as well as Lars Anderson of UC Davis. I also connected with two French *Caulerpa* experts that I had met back in 2002 at the international conference in San Diego: Thierry Thibaut and Alexandre Meinesz. Details were sorted out online, and I was so excited to have an educational component to my Mediterranean adventure.

Thierry was no longer based in Nice, France, but was now with the Mediterranean Institute of Oceanography just outside of Marseille. He told me that *Caulerpa taxifolia* had decreased in some areas, but expanded in others. He invited me to meet his colleagues who were also deeply involved with the *Caulerpa* story. He also informed me of another species, *Caulerpa cylindracea*, which is even worse than *C. taxifolia*: a faster, stronger and deeper invader!

Meanwhile, I connected with Alex and reminded him of the San Diego conference, and of him signing my book (it had been 13 years). Besides, I was *the* Carlsbad city staff representative during the conference. He graciously agreed to meet with me in Nice, and also noted the recent regression of *Caulerpa taxifolia* in some areas. My excitement mounting, I finalized my plans to visit their coastline during the last few days of September and first few days of October 2015. I also made contact with Lars Anderson and asked him for thoughts on the regression of *Caulerpa*, since I had also recently read that some areas in Australia experienced regression. Was this situation still serious? Was my story still relevant? Reassured that it certainly was still relevant, the current Mediterranean and Australian realities involve a larger and complex dynamic of understanding invasive species, which is still being experienced at the very earliest levels.

The rapid, explosive growth of invasive species has also been documented with subsequent declines. However, every place and situation varies. These cycles of growth and decline are neither wholesale nor guaranteed; they do not occur everywhere or every time, as some areas experience continued occupation by invasive species. In addition, with a reduced or reversed presence of an invasive species, some cases nevertheless reveal a lasting, significant impact to the natural baseline of biodiversity of a given area. Through online research and readings, I came across Daniel Simberloff of the Department of Ecology and Evolutionary Biology with the University of Tennessee. Turns out he worked with Alex Meinesz to translate *Killer Algae* into English, and responded to my query about *Caulerpa taxifolia* regression in the Mediterranean with some very insightful input. First, he noted that while *Caulerpa taxifolia* has regressed in some areas, *Caulerpa racemosa* has taken off in others.

Second, some invasive species maintain a low profile or presence for some time, and then suddenly explode or collapse when the proper ecological trigger occurs after an initial, invasive establishment. Other situations involve a failure of an invasive species to get established, while some locations see a major invasion by the same species. He forwarded a 2004 paper that he co-authored in the journal *Biological Invasion*: "Now You See Them, Now You Don't!—Population Crashes of Established Introduced Species." Regarding the relevancy of attacking invasive species in a timely and effective manner, and related funding and policy efforts, the paper made one point clear, which Anderson and others had also voiced. With regards to cycles of growth and regression, or even spontaneous collapse, the paper states, "The possibility of such an event is unwarranted as a potential rationale for a do-nothing approach to management. For such species, even if a crash ultimately occurs, the species may already have caused permanent ecological damage."

Therefore, I was convinced even more that the story of Carlsbad's *Caulerpa* conquest indeed remains worthy, important, and relevant.

With a huge amount of excitement, yet humbled with awe and renewed respect for the work of marine scientists and coastal policy managers everywhere, I set out on the trip. My itinerary involved an initial week on the Grand Canal in Venice, where I would experience stand-up paddling in addition to culture and history; then Rome for more culture and history at the ancient sites, the Colosseum, and the Vatican. I planned five full days between Marseille and Nice/Monaco, and then a visit to the island of Sardinia.

It felt like a date with destiny to further my understanding of *Caulerpa taxifolia*, to advance my love of the ocean, to be thrilled by the wonders of the world, and to be able to conclude my writings after my Mission to Monaco.

Chapter 12
September 2015: Mission to Monaco

Monaco, the French Riviera, and the Mediterranean Sea. Images of calm blue waters are easily conjured at the mention of these locations, and for good reason. I eagerly anticipated my visit to the coastline of the "rich and famous," and to learn more about the current condition of *Caulerpa taxifolia*.

I made prior arrangements to visit Dr. Thierry Thibaut for a day at the Mediterranean Institute of Oceanography (MIO) Luminy Campus, between Marseille and Cassis on the southern coast of France. Afterward, my plan was to journey up the coast to Monaco to visit the Oceanographic Museum and also Alex Meinesz, now Professor Emeritus at the University of Nice Sophia Antipolis. Thierry was a former student of Alex's with much experience and expertise regarding *Caulerpa taxifolia*, seaweeds, phycology, invasive species, and related topics. While we had briefly met in San Diego in 2002, I was honored to schedule time with him.

Cassis is a charming small French Riviera town on the Mediterranean coast, with green trees, blue waters, white limestone cliffs, beige massifs, and a village embracing a quaint boat harbor. It is located 20 minutes from the MIO and university campus at Luminy, separated by a pleasant drive with stunning Mediterranean views and landscapes. When the weather became unsettled during my stay, preventing the opportunity to snorkel with Thierry, we spent a full afternoon at the MIO facility, where I was able to meet some of his colleagues, tour the site, and discuss *Caulerpa taxifolia* and current ocean-research programs. Visiting one of the largest centers for ocean research in Europe was an incredible experience, and provided a great setting to discuss ocean issues, which carried over into our dinner discussions later that night at a seafront restaurant on the bay of Marseille.

Here is what I learned: The Mediterranean faces many ocean and coastal resource challenges, including invasive species, impacts from global warming, and deforestation. To a degree, all these issues are related and further challenged by human action such as overfishing, pollution, shipping, and the corresponding effects of ballast water intake and discharges. *Caulerpa taxifolia* is not choking the life out of the Mediterranean by itself; rather, it is part of a complex matrix of environmental problems and situations taxing the efforts of concerned policy managers, scientists including MIO researchers, and governmental agencies.

At the MIO, I felt like I stood at ground zero of a war zone command center. Scientific research, public outreach, and a constant quest for understanding served as the foundation of the MIO mission. Invasive species can have no enemies. Understanding the source of various invaders and deciphering their cycles of growth, location, regression, and regrowth can be baffling for the scientists and researchers involved.

Something became very clear to me: the challenge of dealing with two issues unfamiliar to this visiting American, and the level at which these French scientists confront it on a daily basis. One is the mass migrant movements from North Africa and the Middle East, particularly Syria, across the Mediterranean to Southern Europe. The other is terrorism fueled by radical Islam. These two realities compete for the attention of the general public in countries that border the Mediterranean Sea, and in fact most of the European continent. Significant national immigration policy debates, funding polemics, and public unrest confront these countries daily, and in turn dilute the ability to apply attention and resources to solving environmental problems on their coastlines and within the Mediterranean Sea.

The January 7, 2015, Charlie Hebdo terror attack in Paris, France, was quite fresh with MIO researchers as they somberly explained how hard it is to solve ocean environmental problems when daily life in their public streets is at risk. Securing public concern and awareness, let alone adequate funding, clearly puts the management of marine resources on the back burner. I wondered how our *Caulerpa* eradication efforts would have progressed if we were in a similar situation. It created a much larger perspective and appreciation to view their efforts for ocean research and establishing programs, such as marine preserves, given the daily threat of terrorism, violence, and disruption. A mere six weeks after my visit, the multi-pronged Paris terror attacks of November 13, 2015, reinforced that reality.

I met two of Thierry's MIO colleagues, Dr. Sandrine Ruitton and Dr. Marc Verlaque. Like Thierry, they were phycologists, experts in aquatic botany, including native and invasive seaweeds. Through research, publications, videos, and other public outreach media, they bring their scientific findings to a wide audience to promote awareness for global warming, invasive species impacts, and the benefits of marine preserves. They shared recent research efforts, visual presentations, and video clips of underwater marine life. In fact, Marc was part of a research team that published two articles documenting the Mediterranean expansion of *Caulerpa taxifolia*: (1) the December 15, 2014, online publication of BioInvasions Records ("It Was Only a Matter of Time: Occurrence of *Caulerpa taxifolia* in the Maltese Islands"), outlined the first detection of *Caulerpa taxifolia* in Malta, the small island nation south of Sicily. It cited the likely vector for invasion as recreational and/or commercial shipping; (2) the June 8, 2015, online publication of *Aquatic Invasions* ("Further Expansion of the Alien Seaweed *Caulerpa taxifolia* in the Eastern Mediterranean Sea") outlined the continued detection in Cyprus, and the first detection in Greece (Rhodes Island). It noted *C. taxifolia*'s potential to become a major pest, and reported detection to at least 100 meters (approximately 328 feet), the deepest record of an alien *Caulerpa* in the Mediterranean Sea. The story is still unfolding over time.

What really impressed me was the extensive MIO library collection of algae and seaweed samples from Mediterranean waters. I viewed seaweed samples dating back to the 1700s and the time of King Louis XIV, with handwritten notes and hand-drawn detail of the samples collected. There were books with pages and pages of algae drawings and actual samples attached to the pages from hundreds of years ago, long before the modern digital photography era that now captures high-resolution images instantly for computer viewing and video clips.

More recent samples from the period around the 1960s included samples from the *Calypso*, the research vessel captained by the renowned Jacques Cousteau. This brought up the inevitable discussion about Cousteau, his tenure at the Monaco Oceanographic Museum, and the alleged aquarium release of *Caulerpa taxifolia* into adjacent waters. Also discussed was the impact of scuba diving, which led to sustained underwater spear fishing. This, combined with the extensive culling of marine life and corresponding collection methods under Cousteau's watch, resulted in the killing of much sea life. No one can question the educational aspect of these efforts for the general public, nor does anyone seriously question Cousteau's role as a modern godfather of marine ecology. Yet, I sensed another sentiment that was almost in awe of the collateral damage that also occurred back then.

I was introduced to two camps among Mediterranean scientists and the *Caulerpa* puzzle. There was the "pure science" camp led by Meinesz, a French scientist who originated from the Netherlands, and the Monaco establishment-sponsored camp led by Dr. Jean Jaubert. A whole book could be written just on these two camps and their corresponding claims, concerns, and citations of conspiracy to promote their cause and credibility. Meinesz wrote *Killer Algae* about his story to initiate change and mobilize a response to early *Caulerpa* concerns, during which Jaubert and Monaco aquarium directors were ready to counterpunch every effort.

Two Saudi Arabian mega yacht vessels (*Golden Odyssey* and *Golden Shadow*), owned by Saudi Prince Khaled, are described in the 2003 version of *Killer Algae*. These were also brought to my attention during my visit, since both had on-board aquariums, designed under the oversight of Professor Jaubert. I would learn more about half-held thoughts on *Caulerpa* infestations later, during my time with Meinesz. But even in Marseille while talking with Thierry and his MIO colleagues, the coincidence of known *Caulerpa taxifolia* in those onboard aquariums was pointed out to me relative to the distribution of *Caulerpa taxifolia*, which in cases spanned the Mediterranean basin in a manner that complicated a clear scientific basis for the explanation of its far-flung geographic presence.

Focusing back on the current status of *Caulerpa taxifolia*, I heard again of another species providing a greater threat than *taxifolia*: *Caulerpa racemosa*. *Caulerpa racemosa* shares a similar genetic relationship with the temperate cold water, West Coast Australia-Perth strain.

Caulerpa racemosa and variation strain *Caulerpa cylindracea*, so named due to its morphology that resembles sea grapes, was first found approximately six years after *Caulerpa taxifolia*. No one really knows how it entered the Mediterranean, whether via ballast water from ships, or incoming currents associated with the Suez Canal, a known transportation corridor for invasive marine species into the Mediterranean. Built by Egypt in the 1860s to create a far shorter international shipping (and war vessel) shortcut, the Suez Canal was cited as a source for the presence of *Caulerpa taxifolia* by the Monaco camp—in opposition to the idea of an aquarium release.

MIO researcher and *Caulerpa* expert Marc Verlaque co-authored a Marine Pollution Bulletin for Science Direct in 2008 ("The *Caulerpa Racemosa* Invasion: A Critical Review") outlining the threat of this alien alga. It noted that the invasion could be considered one of the most serious in the history of species introduced into the Mediterranean Sea, but has not garnered the attention of the famous "killer alga" *Caulerpa taxifolia.*

Regardless of how *Caulerpa racemosa* got established, it poses a far greater threat to biodiversity because of the difference in reproductive patterns. While *Caulerpa taxifolia* reproduces from fragmentation, *Caulerpa racemosa* reproduces sexually. This is significant. *Caulerpa taxifolia* can spread up to a square meter, or about 10.7 square feet, by the second year of growth. However, *Caulerpa racemosa* can spread up to a hectare, or about 107,593 square feet, by the second year of growth—10,000 times greater. Fragmentation requires a physical fragment to detach from the main body of the alga, or seaweed plant. Sexual reproduction requires specific seasonal conditions and timing, about five minutes before sunset with water temperatures at 21 degrees Celsius (70 degrees Fahrenheit). Compared to fragmentation, sexual reproduction represents an explosive form of new growth with a vast areal extent of possible coverage. It also extends into deep water, ranging from the surface to 60 meters (about 200 feet), with the densest area around 30 to 60 meters (100 to 200 feet).

Thus, *Caulerpa taxifolia* and *Caulerpa racemosa/cylindracea* are included on the list of worst alien invaders for the Mediterranean Sea. They comprise a portion of the matrix of environmental problems there. In addition to pollution, global warming, and overfishing, the emerging issue of deforestation is getting the attention of MIO researchers. Deforestation (the reduction of underwater biomass) impacts include habitat loss, marine nursery loss, and carbon loss. One result is that seafloor areas devoid of native biomass and *Posidonia* grasses become barren turf areas. These, in turn, can facilitate the introduction and colonization of invasive species. Conversely, seabed areas occupied by native seaweed like *Posidonia* can help limit invasive species like *Caulerpa taxifolia* and *racemosa* by acting as barriers. Thus, establishing marine preserves and sanctuaries are a current focus of the MIO team.

Also made clear to me was how global warming was not an idea, but a scientific fact. One study undertaken on the north coast of Spain confirmed global warming's impact on coastal waters, which resulted in large-scale deforestation over a scale of 200+ kilometers (approximately 124 miles). Deforestation reduces the ability for the oceans to sequester carbon and contributes to the cycle of continued global warming. Of course, invasive species that temporarily, seasonally, or even permanently displace native biomass can add to the impact of deforestation. In addition, warming ocean waters may help promote the sustained presence of invasive species such as the mutant genetic clone of *Caulerpa taxifolia.*

The complexity of ocean resource understanding and related management issues that exist in the Mediterranean Sea was quite an eye-opener for me. It stretched far beyond the singular *Caulerpa taxifolia* challenge we faced in Carlsbad. Dredging, poison, and dynamite practices affect fishery resources; in addition, regional conflicts around the southern and eastern shorelines of the Mediterranean perimeter, as well as other coastal areas, were also cited as challenges by MIO researchers. For example, the first Persian Gulf War of the early 1990s created research barriers and greatly restricted access for scientists. In retrospect, that prevented the development of historical baseline conditions from which to assess biodiversity change over time.

What will happen over time? That remains a mystery. Which impacts can be attributed to *Caulerpa taxifolia* alone? Which have occurred in combination with other environmental factors? The MIO team enjoyed my 2014 TED video about *Caulerpa taxifolia* and the resource that it provides as an outreach tool via its informative, short, and animated format. The one point of absolute certainty, collectively voiced by Thierry and his MIO colleagues, was that the Agua Hedionda Lagoon eradication remains an important and inspirational success story.

With my head swirling with information, knowledge, and questions, I pointed my focus toward Nice and Monaco, where I wanted to see the Aquarium, visit Alex Meinesz, and hopefully observe the mysterious *Caulerpa taxifolia* in Mediterranean waters with my own eyes.

Touring the Monaco Oceanographic Museum

My next three days included a visit to the aquarium at the Monaco Oceanographic Museum, connecting with Alex for an attempt to snorkel and see *Caulerpa taxifolia*, and then reconvening for dinner on the third day before flying out to Sardinia the following day. This schedule was based on a hopeful window of good weather and ocean conditions forecast for the second day. My hotel was within the very upscale harbor at Cap D'Ail, technically located on the French coast but literally a stone's throw from the Monaco border, with all the flash and fuss that comes with one of the world's richest and smallest sovereign states.

Driving from Cassis to Nice was quite beautiful, but the ocean was in complete unrest. As I neared the coast in southern Nice, the ocean churned with amazing wind-whipped whitecaps as far as the eye could see to the horizon. Gale-force northeast winds blew with staggering intensity. I thought to myself, "The ocean is death today." Nevertheless, the excitement of entering Monaco mounted, and upon seeing the Oceanographic Museum perched on its clifftop location, my anticipation was boiling over.

After taking photos of the museum as it loomed dramatically over the surging Mediterranean waters, we entered. Built by Prince Albert I in the early 1900s, around the same time as the Panama Canal construction, it clearly reflected his desire to erect a temple of respect for the ocean he deeply loved. Exhibits cover his activities as an exploring oceanographer. Conference halls contain other exhibits of marine life. On the lower level is the aquarium. Enormous windows dramatically framed the Mediterranean Sea horizon with stunning visual impact. For this ocean lover, the Oceanographic Museum is truly an inspiring temple celebrating the power and mysteries of the sea.

I was fully enthralled with the aquarium exhibits and the prolific displays of fish, sharks, and other marine life that replicated various natural environments for public viewing and education. I was swept away with the colors, movements, and presence of the marine plants and animal life on display. After a while, though, my thoughts returned to the *Caulerpa taxifolia* situation. As I reflected back to its early history as an invader in the early 1980s, I could see an innocent aspect to the release of aquarium water that may have initially stirred this dangerous pot. What did not seem so understanding and innocent was the subsequent response (or lack thereof) by aquarium directors and government agencies, as documented in *Killer Algae*. They downplayed any serious impacts, diverted attention, and even questioned the credibility of those raising a vocal alarm of awareness.

After again reminding myself that the once domineering presence of *Caulerpa taxifolia* had regressed, I prepared for that inevitable moment I had visualized for so long: to ask an aquarium staff person about *Caulerpa taxifolia*. There were a few different staff members in the aquarium area, mainly tending to maintenance duties as they popped in and out of various doors and hallways. I selected one that seemed to have sun on his face, which for me translated into someone that enters the ocean often. He seemed to be an established staff person, not a new hire that may not know about the *Caulerpa* situation.

I stopped him and said, in very slow English, that I had a question. (I only know about four words in French.) Also, I have learned while traveling over the years that my appearance and voice readily give away my California origin. In his slow English, with a thick French accent, he and I engaged in a moment or two of small talk. Our eye contact and facial demeanor were very relaxed and comfortable until I said, "I understand that about ten years ago or more there was a problem with *Caulerpa taxifolia*, and perhaps it came from the aquarium. How is that situation now?"

"I am very sorry, but I do not understand your English," he said, in his French-accented but perfectly stated English.

After repeating the phrase "*Caulerpa taxifolia*" several times, figuring it was not subject to linguistic translation, just voice and accent parameters, he stated that it was a problem years ago, but not anymore. Furthermore, he added, the aquarium no longer used or displayed *Caulerpa taxifolia*. Satisfied, I felt bad for creating a moment of discomfort. Alex later told me that he, the preeminent authority on the subject, was essentially barred from entry into the aquarium back in the day of *Caulerpa* conflicts and debates. The staff seemed prepared with a packaged response in the event they received a query like mine. I definitely was in the home territory of the Monaco camp.

Another thing I learned about Monaco is the element of control that permeates everywhere and everything: control of traffic flow, control of pedestrian circulation, control of dress code, control of hours of operation and manners of access, control of visitation, control of speed limits, control of protocols, control of law enforcement, control of parking allowances, control of beach and water access. And control of public image. I could see retroactively how the message of *Caulerpa* was handled in the manner described by Alex in *Killer Algae*. It made a lot of sense to me. Monaco is known as being "beautiful," in an urban beach, high-density sort of way. However, the coastline is not particularly pristine, and marine resources are at peril from development, pollution, and other typical challenges that an intensely built and utilized shoreline anywhere would face.

In this culture of "control," Monaco-supported scientists, aquarium directors, public agency staff, media outlets, and others could be swept into a larger context of producing and providing comfortable and reassuring public messages of environmental concern and marine resource protection. The mechanics of the Monaco aquarium camp made sense to me, just as the mechanics of the other camp made sense as well. Every story has at least two sides, and with *Caulerpa taxifolia* now being part of a larger matrix of environmental problems for the Mediterranean Sea, it is a complex task to point a finger and isolate cause, effect, and blame.

Chapter 13
October 2015: Snorkeling with the Enemy

The postcard-perfect peninsula of Saint Jean Cap Ferrat extends perpendicularly from the shoreline west of Monaco along the French Riviera coastline. This area and the Cap Ferrat peninsula comprise one of the most affluent areas in this upscale region. It features beautiful Mediterranean vistas, narrow roads, palatial and stylish homes, greenways, open space, shoreline parks and trails, pocket beaches, azure waters, and a bustling but not overworked yacht harbor with commercial and eating establishments. It is easily a version of Mediterranean bliss for those lucky enough to live or visit there.

Alex made an appointment for our rendezvous on Thursday, October 1 at one of the protected bays at the head of the peninsula, which provided relatively calm waters from the winds and rough seas that had subsided greatly overnight. Here, I would have my best opportunity to view *Caulerpa taxifolia* with one of the most experienced and qualified experts in the world. To say I was excited is a comical understatement.

The bottom of the bay was once covered with *Caulerpa taxifolia*. The presence of the invasive seaweed was so prevalent that it became the site of various graduate-level research studies for some of Alex's past students, including Thierry Thibaut. However, per Alex, there was nearly no *Caulerpa* present in June 2015. In preparation for my visit, he returned in mid-September and saw *Caulerpa* making a reemergence of sorts. The explanation of the local regression is not really understood, and highlights a larger issue of not being able to fully understand ecosystem changes and adjustments brought about by invasive species. The baseline conditions become altered and prediction becomes elusive. Only over time and by reviewing responses in the field can attempts be made to solve the puzzle.

Two possible theories of regression were suggested by Alex. The first has to do with the unique genetic makeup of the invasive strain of *Caulerpa taxifolia*.

Only male gametes (reproductive cells) are involved with reproduction. One idea is that some sort of ecological collapse occurred without the balance of both male and female gametes. The other theory is that periods of growth and regression could be tied to solar cycles. While many cycles are in place regarding solar radiation, the flowering of the local *Posidonia* seagrass is tied to 11-year solar cycles. This is part of a larger field of science known as chronobiology and biological rhythms.

Chronobiology examines cycles in living organisms and their adaption to solar and lunar cycles. This applies to some degree to all living organisms, even at the molecular biological scale. Biological rhythms in response to solar cycles can affect the timing and duration of various activities, including but not limited to cellular regeneration, leaf movements, and photosynthesis. Microbial organisms are also subject to chronobiology such as fungi, protozoa, and even bacteria. These theories might help explain the cycles of *Caulerpa taxifolia* growth, regression, and regrowth independently, in some combination, or perhaps not at all.

But for now, my thoughts were solely focused on viewing the invader that had captured my attention, time, money, and imagination for over 15 years. Alex Meinesz was very patient with me and probably amused at my enthusiasm as well. At our core, I felt we both were comfortable with the fact that we each loved the ocean and valued any time spent on or within it. He lent me snorkel gear, and we waded into the calm, 70-degree waters. No wetsuit was necessary and visibility was quite adequate, although there was more water movement just outside the protected corners of the bay.

I followed Alex as he swam like a fish, kicking with his fins and arms stroking through the water. Swimming perhaps fifty to eighty yards into the middle of the bay and viewing the sandy bottom with occasional rocks and *Posidonia* seagrass, I had my new underwater camera ready to capture images and video of *Caulerpa*. Quite suddenly, I heard Alex call me over with an animated voice and pointed downward.

He had spotted a patch.

After diving down about ten feet, I saw the familiar bright-green leafy *Caulerpa taxifolia*. It was distinctly more green and colorful than the adjacent native seagrass as it popped up through the sediment. Suddenly, all the previous photos and videos that I had seen came to life, in front of my eyes. It shouldn't be a joyful thing to see an invasive species proliferating over an area, I know, but I was sincerely excited and satisfied to finally come face to face with this alien seaweed.

For the next hour or so, we moved about the bay and circled over patches of *Caulerpa taxifolia*, and then dived down for a close look. Some patches were thin, while others occupied the fringes of native seagrass. Still other patches seemed thick and robustly establishing their presence and expansion as the *Caulerpa* leaves swayed back and forth with the currents. It wanted to grow over and around the native seagrass, imposing its bright-green form wherever it could continue its growth pattern. It *looked* like an invader.

Meanwhile, Alex shared my excitement as he repeatedly took my camera and shot underwater video clips and images of the various patches. We also saw *Caulerpa racemosa* and its distinctive sea grape morphology, with little balls attached to its root system. He carefully removed some samples, and later on shore, laid them out on a beach mat and further educated me. After more photos, we dried off in the sun. That triggered our appetites, which we richly satisfied at a nearby harbor eatery with sunny sea views and an amazing seafood salad platter.

Conclusion: Breaking It Down While Looking Ahead

On our final night, I digested what I had learned about *Caulerpa*, and about how humans respond to environmental problems. Between Thierry, his MIO colleagues, and now Alex, I had learned so much. The challenge now would be for me to properly summarize, synthesize, and sort out all the information, memories, and experiences occupying my bursting brain. Alex and the others did not have all the answers, despite so much knowledge and intelligence. How had some invasive species arrived in the Mediterranean? How to explain cycles of growth, expansion, regression, and reemergence? How to explain human-related challenges to become mobilized for concern, policy implementation, funding allocations?

Alex's level of intelligence and insight is really impressive. He had the courage to speak up on behalf of the Mediterranean ocean environment, directly in the hostile face of the Monaco camp and establishment. In 2008, he wrote a book, *How Life Began*; who writes a book like that?

It once again made me realize that environmental and ocean challenges get confronted head-on by high-performing individuals. These people become the leading edge for other human energy and institutional resources that persevere and seek success. They aim to undo the harm to nature created by human nature, by the hand of man. I was reminded of the late Greig Peters, who set the course of our action to collaborate and eradicate the Carlsbad infestation. I thought of David Lloyd, the power plant attorney who mobilized money to initiate combat while most were struggling to find proper footing in the matter. Many people provided inspiring and valuable lessons to me that will last a lifetime: all the SCCAT members and stakeholders; Keith Merkel and his incredible team; Thierry and his MIO colleagues; my own city mayor, the late Bud Lewis; city council, community leaders, mentors and peers; countless community members; lagoon lovers and users; celebrities that took part and became true friends like Christopher Knight and celebrity connection David Mirisch; Australian councillors who met with me; conference attendees and co-speakers; agency staff; scientists from everywhere; and many local Carlsbad surfers who showed constant interest and appreciation for the eradication efforts that kept the lagoon open for boating, paddling, and fishing. It was very inspiring to reconnect with Alex again. The range of topics during our dinner conversation was quite diverse, but often swirled back to *Caulerpa taxifolia*.

During our talk, the two Saudi luxury yachts, the *Golden Odyssey* and *Golden Shadow*, came up again. Apparently, one or both vessels sailed to a shipyard in San Diego Bay more than once for repainting and maintenance. They had various marine species onboard, just like during their other worldwide voyages and Mediterranean presence. Looking at the Mediterranean distribution of *Caulerpa taxifolia* during the mid 1990s, and how it touched some outlying areas (like the Balearic Spanish Mediterranean island of Majorca), was tricky to explain. How about Arabian Sea species that showed up in front of the Monaco Oceanographic Museum? Meanwhile, on-board aquariums were cleaned, and aquaria contents from the luxury yachts (including known *Caulerpa taxifolia* sprigs) were confined to local university laboratories at La Jolla's Scripps Institute of Oceanography near San Diego. In the updated 2003 version of *Killer Algae*, Alex Meinesz clearly states any connection to the Carlsbad infestations are purely coincidental, fictitious, yet intriguing enough to mention in his book.

Prior to American and Australian detections of *Caulerpa taxifolia*, a Japanese phycologist who spent time with Alex in the Mediterranean researched 51 public aquaria throughout Japan. Nearly half had *C. taxifolia*. One aquarium, Enoshima, was constructed by the Museum of Monaco under a patent awarded to Dr. Jaubert. The *Caulerpa* was analyzed and found to be the same genetic clone as the Mediterranean strain. In the summer of 1992, a patch was found near the aquarium's exhaust pipe. This appears to greatly mimic the Mediterranean situation that unfolded at Monaco. The following winter, severely cold water (averaging 8 degrees Celsius/46 degrees Fahrenheit) resulted in the disappearance of *Caulerpa taxifolia*; it did not return the following spring. This case also highlights the larger issue of controlling the alga in aquaria trade circles worldwide, and its continued availability online via the internet.

These are a combination of facts and intriguing intellectual ponderings, and perhaps reflect the battle scars of the differing camps surrounding the *Caulerpa* mystery. Its presence, invasion, and current status all remain true mysteries: unfolding, unsolved, unfinished mysteries.

Alex also cited the Gulf of Lyon on France's south coast, which funnels strong Mistral winds into the Mediterranean (which generate surfable swell for the west coast of Sardinia) and creates upwelling and corresponding cooling of water temperature to the point that *Caulerpa taxifolia* undergoes a seasonal reduction. However, global warming is a new factor, currently measured at approximately 0.2 degrees Celsius per 10 years, so the dynamics of Mediterranean water temperatures relative to invasive species cycles are now in flux. Perhaps over time the seasonal reduction of *Caulerpa taxifolia* may be lessened due to global warming and increased temperatures of Mediterranean waters.

We also discussed the dual threat of *Caulerpa taxifolia* and *C. racemosa*, the latter finding ground in the muddy and disturbed environments of harbor areas. Shipping and ballast water may explain its initial source of invasion. Likewise, the network of Mediterranean harbors with *Caulerpa racemosa* may be linked by commercial shipping traffic and related ballast water movements. Take Italy for example, where I spoke with fisherman and port officials about the presence of *Caulerpa* on the Italian island of Sardinia. Meinesz notes on page 299 of *Killer Algae*: "Indifference, diversions, dissension, allegiances to agencies, and closed fraternities of various specialists and power brokers have thus led to substantial ignorance about this problem in Italy. The result is the same as in France, where eight years of institutional palaver in several official committees have resulted in a situation where there is no control strategy. *Caulerpa taxifolia* has been able to grow unopposed in Italy and for several years it has been impossible to slow its spread."

I now realize that the above passage, if considered in reverse, outlines the formula for the success of Carlsbad's eradication. We lacked indifference and avoided diversion; we sought consensus and practiced allegiance to agency mission statements, not agency protocols or precedents. We did not tolerate any closed fraternities of specialists or power brokers, preventing ignorance and replacing it with collaboration and useful information obtained from the lessons learned by others. We had no institutional palaver. We crafted an effective control strategy. Combined with rapid and timely response, and the geographical benefit of detecting *Caulerpa taxifolia* within a coastal lagoon vs. open ocean location, we found the formula for our success. Hopefully, it will always serve as a template for others.

Not everyone in this world or those living within a short distance of a pressing environmental problem is physically, emotionally, and/or spiritually close to nature. The same can be said for the ocean: not everyone has a meaningful relationship with it. One person's passion and focus may or may not be in alignment with another person, so as to form a majority consensus on forging policy or action in response to an environmental challenge. Often, it is hard to get people to look past their immediate health and wealth, let alone an alien mutant seaweed clone that grows on the ocean bottom and cannot be seen from the surface. Add the elusive challenge of understanding genetically distinct invasive species, and it is easy to see why biological invasions of various diverse forms are altering ecosystems to significant degrees worldwide. These alterations ultimately lead to economic impacts and real threats to quality of life. Of course, by the time there is an economic or social impact, there often is no longer an environmental solution.

Short of a comprehensive, lagoon-wide monitoring effort, funds on the scale of $50,000 could finance a general overview survey including "hot spots" in front of storm drains. Such an allowance within the combined budgets of the city, power plant, desalination plant, agencies, grant programs, and/or other stakeholders would go far to help safeguard the future of the lagoon.

The summer of 2016 marked the ten-year anniversary of our historic and precedent-setting eradication of *Caulerpa taxifolia* from Carlsbad's Agua Hedionda Lagoon.

In closing, if I were to assemble a wide-ranging list of words and phrases that collectively capture the challenge of eradicating an invasive biological species like we did in Carlsbad, there are several I could provide: cultural factors, political forces, the limitations of human nature, non-linear reality, stakeholder, pride, science, precedent, protocol, logic, prioritization of problems, polemic, profit motive, distractions, focus, nonprofit organization, communication, agency, debate, dialogue, funding, consensus, conflict, combat, collaboration, inspiration, conspiracy, diplomacy, delay, deploy, outreach, enforcement, efficacy, frustration, celebration, negotiation, closure, restriction, acceleration, action, concern, convene, control, innovate, attention, legislation, response, regression, expansion, learning curves, team, plan, open-mindedness, threat, rhythm, progress, humor, tragedy, opportunity, milestone, deception, and probably the most important word: perception.

Without the perception of a problem that requires attention, nothing that resembles an effective response can be generated.

Alexandre Meinesz, Thierry and the MIO researchers, in addition to countless others I have met over the years around the coastal world, have made it clear to me over and over again: Carlsbad's successful conquest with eradicating *Caulerpa taxifolia* is a tribute to the best qualities of humans working together to care for the earth, the environment, and the oceans. This story has timeless value and needs to be communicated and memorialized for posterity.

My Mediterranean experience was very powerful, moving, and captivating. It was a source of inspiration, education, and actualization. While all coastal areas in every ocean warrant our attention, care, and respect, the Mediterranean Sea possesses for me a timeless dimension serving as the cradle of ancient civilizations. Yet it is currently under the strain of very modern and significant environmental challenges. While environmental problems may have different forms and scales around the world, it is the nature of the human response that can promote aid or harm.

Coastal lagoons are the bridge between the land and the sea. Coastal lagoon stewardship, therefore, requires an understanding of the earth and the humans that occupy it, as well as the oceans and the marine life that reside within it.

When we talk about saving the world, surely saving the oceans represents a true path. And if saving the oceans begins with one patch of water at a time, then saving Agua Hedionda Lagoon was a great place to start.

Because at the end of the day, no ocean = no hope.

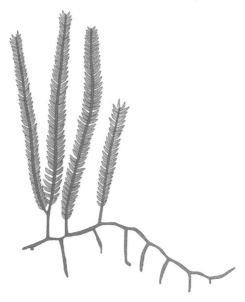

1.

2A.

Destructive Seaweed Threatens California

Caulerpa taxifolia

If you see it, immediately report it, but DO NOT disturb it!

2B.

ATTENTION

A team of SCUBA divers is working throughout Agua Hedionda Lagoon to search for and eradicate the invasive exotic seaweed *Caulerpa taxifolia*. The divers are accompanied by one to two boats flying dive flags (see above and below). For your safety and the safety of the divers, please do not pass your vessel or towed passenger within 200 feet of any dive flags. For current information on survey locations and temporary area closures, please call (760) 439-1023 or visit the internet site, www.caulerpa.cjb.net

3.

HELP

AGUA HEDIONDA LAGOON MAY BE CLOSED TO RECREATION FOREVER

(Carlsbad, CA November 8, 2001)

We recently learned that the Southern California Caulerpa Action Team (SCCAT), will request the Carlsbad City Council to close the Agua Hedionda lagoon to all recreational boating as a necessary step in eradication of the foreign algae. SCCAT is a quasi-governmental committee involved with eradication of the so-called "killer algae"(Caulerpa taxifolia). They will be present next Tuesday evening (6:00 p.m. November 13th at Council Chambers) to make their recommendation. Apparently efforts over the past one and one half years have been over 95 percent effective in eliminating the Caulerpa. However, several additional contaminated sites have recently been found through the first extensive survey conducted since the Caulerpa was first discovered about one and one half years ago.

Bristol Cove Property Owners Association and a host of other entities involved with recreational use in the lagoon strongly support the rapid and complete removal of this noxious algae from their "back yard." However, we have been provided almost no information and are not convinced that the best methods of eradication are being employed, nor are we convinced that complete closing of the lagoon to boating is essential. To this end, Bristol Cove is retaining experts and seeking answers.

Please support your community and more than 50 years of boating on the lagoon by attending next Tuesday's City Council meeting. We have arranged for several speakers to concisely present our position to the Council.

LATE BREAKING NEWS: "We just received word that the CA Dept. of Fish and Game will delay the matter before the City Council next Tuesday, November 13th. However, they will still be there and so should we. Tell a friend!"

4.

Eradication Technique – Tarps Injected with Chlorine

5.

6.

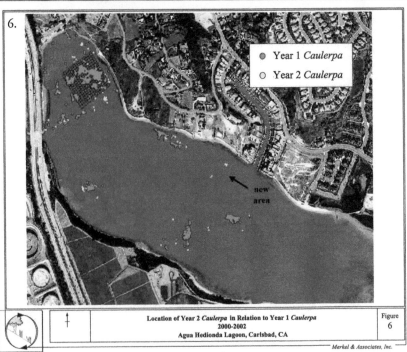

○ Year 1 *Caulerpa*

○ Year 2 *Caulerpa*

new area

Location of Year 2 *Caulerpa* in Relation to Year 1 *Caulerpa*
2000-2002
Agua Hedionda Lagoon, Carlsbad, CA

Figure 6

Merkel & Associates, Inc.

7.

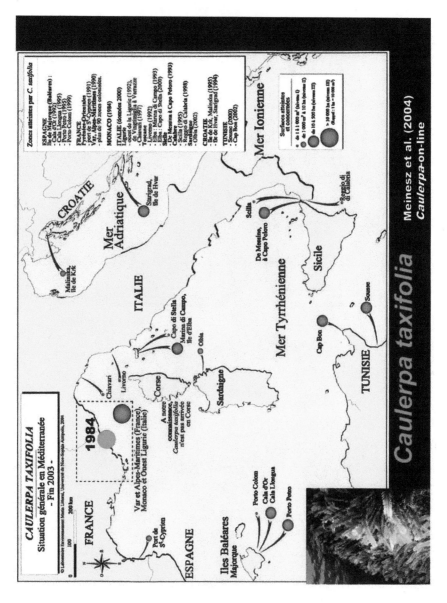

8.

9.

10.

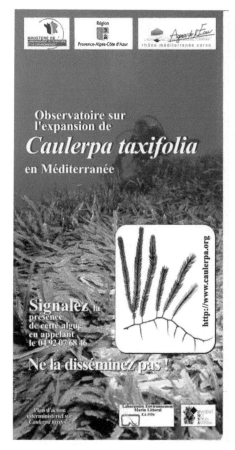

Wanted
Caulerpa taxifolia

If you find this seaweed,
do not help it to spread,
but phone us at: 33 (0)4 92 07 68 46

11.

Caulerpa taxifolia - First report of its introduction to eastern Australia

PHOTO: UPPER: Scanned herbarium specimen is about 11 cm high (From stolon to top of fronds). Photo: Alan Millar - Royal Botanic Gardens, Sydney.
LOWER: *C. taxifolia* in eastern Australian waters. Photo: Neville Coleman - World of Water.

RELATED TOPIC: *C. taxifolia* - introductions worldwide

DIVER ALERT

An invasive, cold-water tolerant strain of the green macroalga *Caulerpa taxifolia* has been confirmed as growing in New South Wales waters. Unknown from mainland New South Wales, Australia, since records began with European settlement, we believe the NSW populations have been here for 5-15 years. This introduction is almost certainly the result of human activity. NSW Fisheries officers Markus Miller and Jack Hannan initially discovered the outbreak and sent specimens to Dr Alan Millar at the Botanic Gardens in Sydney for identification. This was confirmed by Prof. Alexandre Meinesz (University

of Nice), who received specimens from Dr Millar, and has been involved with the outbreak in the Mediterranean since the late 1980s.

146

12.

13.

14.

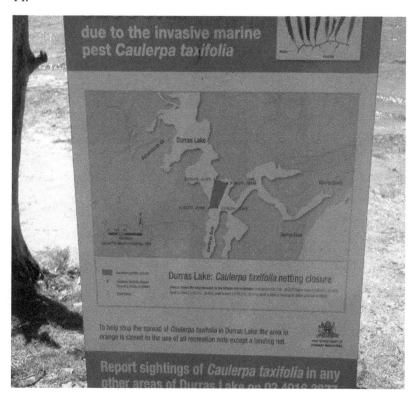

15.

16.

17.

18.

19A.

19B.

20.

21.

22.

23.

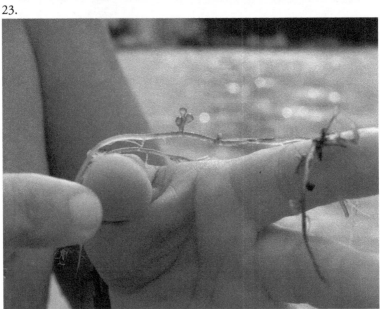

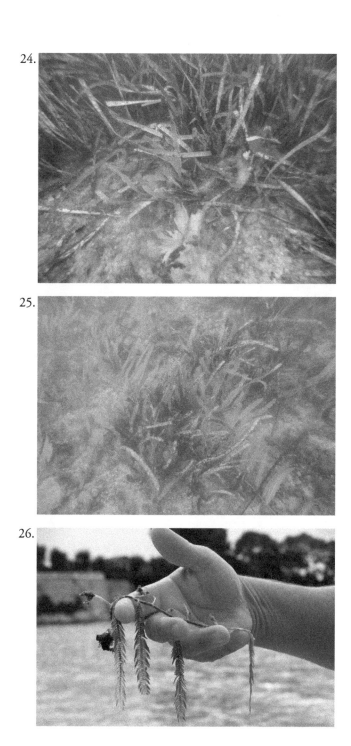

24.

25.

26.

27.

154

28.

29.

It happened before.
It can happen again.

Don't let this ...

turn into this ...

Help prevent a *Caulerpa* invasion.
Be responsible. Don't use it.

If this saltwater aquarium plant gets into our coastal waters,
it can smother native plant and animal life.
Dispose of aquarium plants, animals, and water properly.

Visit **www.sccat.net** to see pictures of the banned *Caulerpa* species.

southern california
caulerpa action team

Photo credits: #0817.11 c Mark Conlin seapics.com; J.M. Cottalorda

Photo Captions

All photos/images by author Eric Muñoz unless otherwise specified.

Page 4. Coastal Research, Sardinia—Italy, 2015 (image by Lizzie Muñoz)

Page 6. Mediterranean Wave, 2015 (image by Lizzie Muñoz)

Page 12.

    Top photo: Christopher Knight and Author, Agua Hedionda Lagoon Foundation Discovery Center, Lagoon Day, 2011 (image Muñoz Collection);

    Bottom photo: Christopher Knight and Carlsbad City Council Proclamation: Lagoon Day, July 2012—Left to right: Mayor Matt Hall, Council member Mark Packard, Christopher Knight, Eric Muñoz, Dave Billings [Buena Vista Lagoon], Council member Ann Kulchin, Council member Farrah Douglas, Fred Sandquist [Batiquitos Lagoon], and Council member Keith Blackburn (image by City of Carlsbad)

Page 16. Alex Meinesz and Author, Cap Ferrat, France, 2015 (image by Lizzie Muñoz)

Page 108. Split Waterfront, Croatia, 2007

Numbered section

1. Aerial View of Agua Hedionda Lagoon (image by Google Earth)
2. #2A: Cover of *Caulerpa taxifolia* outreach brochure (image by sccat.net)
   #2B: Warning sign for dive team
3. HELP Flyer by homeowners association
4. Tarp Eradication Method (image by Rachel Woodfield/Merkel & Associates)
5. Hoover Street Storm Drain; area of initial infestation
6. AHL Status Map: Year 1 vs. Year 2 (image by Rachel Woodfield/Merkel & Associates)
7. Map of *Caulerpa taxifolia* in Mediterranean Sea—2004 (image by Meinesz)
8. Rachel Woodfield and Keith Merkel with Author at 2008 Fishing Event
9. Carlsbad Mayor Bud Lewis with Author: Eradication Day 2006 (image by Lizzie Muñoz)
10. French and English brochures (images by Meinesz)
11. Australian brochure (image by nsw.gov.au)
12. Coastal Research: South Coast NSW Australia (image by Lizzie Muñoz)
13. Australian fisherman with *Caulerpa taxifolia* (image by *Herald Sun*, Australia)
14. Durras Lake map of *Caulerpa taxifolia*—South Coast NSW Australia
15. Gold Coast Councillors Robbins and Douglas with Author (image by Lizzie Muñoz)
16. Lake Conjola sign—South Coast NSW Australia (image by Lizzie Muñoz)
17. 2011 Paddle Regatta Event—Agua Hedionda Lagoon
18. Christopher Knight, David Mirisch, and Author: Lagoon Day 2012 (image by Lizzie Muñoz)

About the Author

Eric Noel Muñoz had various roles with the eradication of *Caulerpa taxifolia* from Carlsbad's Agua Hedionda Lagoon in California. As a Carlsbad city staff planner, he served as a liaison between the community and the multi-agency Southern California *Caulerpa* Action Team. As president and board member of the Agua Hedionda Lagoon Foundation he promoted outreach events. A native of coastal Southern California, he is a lifelong ocean lover with a physical geography degree from San Diego State University. While maintaining an ongoing fondness for Baja California, he has visited various American, foreign, and Mediterranean locations to experience and explore other coastlines and cultures. He has made numerous public, school, community, and conference presentations, and is a TED-Educator with an animated video on *Caulerpa taxifolia*.

Eric has served on the board of directors for the California Shore and Beach Preservation Association with coastal engineers, researchers, agency staff members, and planners; and also is serving as vice-president for the California Surf Museum in Oceanside. He is committed to promoting awareness for coastal environmental issues worldwide.

To contact the author: eric@pacificoceanart.com

Indonesia, 2005 (Image by Teddy Hubbard)

Above: Sardinia, 2015; Below: Venice, 2015
(Images by Lizzie Muñoz)

www.aguahedionda.org

November

Once again, Carlsbad's KILLER ALGAE!!! makes Thornhill's Year In Review.

Some people say Carlsbad is snooty. Some say the city is too sophisticated.

But any burg that stocks killer algae in its lagoons can't be all that uptight.

Eric Munoz

City of Carlsbad

International *Caulerpa taxifolia* Conference

CPSIA information can be obtained
at www.ICGtesting.com
Printed in the USA
LVHW010527060820
662473LV00020B/2233